ECONOMIC ANALYSIS OF REGULATED MARKETS

Economic Analysis of Regulated Markets is urgently needed as a guide to policy-makers and as a collection of rigorous scientific approaches for researchers and students. It provides careful analysis of the interaction between government intervention and competitive market forces.

The failure of government policy in the US railway and airline industry is well known. The book therefore focuses on the deregulation process and its success. The insights should be of general interest for the design of deregulation policies.

A comprehensive set of studies on insurance markets is presented. The groundwork for the understanding of such markets with incomplete information is laid by two theoretical contributions followed by an empirical and a normative analysis of market performance.

The final chapter of the book investigates the impact of regulatory policy on pharmaceutical markets. Price regulations are shown to affect investment adversely – and in addition price ceilings in one country lead to price increases in non-regulating countries. Thus regulatory policies may have adverse effects on consumers outside the regulating country.

Dr Jörg Finsinger, the editor, is Research Fellow at the International Institute of Management, Berlin. He has contributed articles on theoretical and applied microeconomics as well as on competition policy to professional publications.

ECONOMIC ANALYSIS OF REGULATED MARKETS

Edited by
Jörg Finsinger
Research Fellow
International Institute of Management, Berlin

Foreword by
Bernhard Gahlen
Director
International Institute of Management, Berlin

St. Martin's Press   New York

© Jörg Finsinger 1983

All rights reserved. For information, write:
St. Martin's Press, Inc., 175 Fifth Avenue, New York, NY 10010
Printed in Hong Kong
First published in the United States of America in 1983

ISBN 0–312–22682–9

Library of Congress Cataloging in Publication Data

Main entry under title:

Economic analysis of regulated markets.

    Contents: Markets and regulatory policy in
international perspective / Jörg Finsinger—
Pricing issues in the deregulation of railroad
rates / William J. Baumol and Robert D. Willig—
On the contestability of airline markets /
Elizabeth E. Bailey, Daniel P. Kaplan, and David S.
Sibley—[etc.]
    1. Trade regulation—Addresses, essays, lec-
tures. 2. Competition—Addresses, essays, lec-
tures.   I. Finsinger, Jörg.
HD3612. E25 1983   381′.3   82–5769
ISBN 0–312–22682–9   AACR2

For my parents

Contents

Foreword

The contributions to this book were presented at the Regulation Conference and during the subsequent Regulation Workshop held at the International Institute of Management of the Science Centre, Berlin, 1–15 July 1981. The conference was supported by a generous grant from the Thyssen Foundation, for which we are extremely grateful.

The objective of the conference was twofold: first, it provided an opportunity for the exchange of the latest developments in economic research on an international level. Secondly, by emphasizing policy-relevant research it was intended to be of help to decision-makers. For the most part, this conference volume contains papers focusing on current issues in economic policy. Often, government policies are criticized and policy changes are suggested. Of course, in some cases the papers in this volume give only indirect guidance for decision-makers. At times, it is demonstrated only that current regulatory policies lead to outcomes quite different from policy objectives. But such insights are none the less useful.

This book is designed to promote the economics of regulation in Europe. In the US the economics of regulation has long been one of the central applications of microeconomics. The book contains work dealing with US regulatory policy as well as with European issues. It also contains some details on regulatory institutions not available elsewhere. It should be stimulating reading on both sides of the Atlantic.

I would like to thank Dr Jörg Finsinger, Research Fellow at the International Institute of Management, for organizing the conference and the workshop. He also edited this book. Furthermore, I want to thank our staff, especially our secretary, Gisela Spivey, for her patient assistance during the conference preparation and accomplishment.

Berlin   BERNHARD GAHLEN

Notes on the Contributors

Michael Adams studied law and then economics. From 1970 until 1976 he was on the scientific staff of the Institute for Civil Law at the University of Bonn. He worked at the University of Hagen from 1976 until 1978. He was assistant to Professor C. C. von Weizsäcker at the Institute for Social Sciences and Economics at the University of Bonn. He is now at Bern University and his current research is focused on the economics of law.

Elizabeth E. Bailey is Vice-Chairman of the US Civil Aeronautics Board, appointed to that position by President Reagan in 1981. She has served as a Member of the Civil Aeronautics Board since the summer of 1977, after being appointed to the Board by President Carter. Before that she was head of the Economics Research Department at Bell Laboratories and an adjunct associate professor in the Economics Department of New York University. Her studies of economic regulation include *Economic Theory of Regulatory Constraint*. She is chairperson of the Committee on the Status of Women in the Economics Profession, and is an elected member of the Executive Committee of the American Economic Association. She is also a member of the Board of Trustees of Princeton University.

William J. Baumol is Professor of Economics at Princeton and New York Universities. He holds a degree of BSS from the City University of New York (1942) and a PhD from London University (1949). He has taught at Princeton since 1949 and at New York since 1971. He is past-president of the American Economic Association, the Eastern Economic Association and the Association of Environmental and Resource Economists. Among his publications are *Welfare Economics and the Theory of the State, Business Behavior Value and Growth, The Theory of Environmental Policy* (with W. E. Oates) and *Contestable Markets and the Theory of Industry Structure* (with John Panzar and Robert Willig (forthcoming)).

Daniel P. Kaplan is Director of the US Office of Economic Analysis of the Civil Aeronautics Board. He has written and directed a number of studies on the effects of deregulation on the domestic US airline industry.

Paul R. Kleindorfer is Professor of Decision Sciences and Economics at the University of Pennsylvania. He received his doctorate from Carnegie-Mellon University and has published widely in the fields of systems theory, management science and public utility economics. His current research is in the area of public utility pricing and regulation under uncertainty and on consumer choice processes and regulation in insurance markets.

Howard Kunreuther is Professor of Decision Sciences at Wharton School, University of Pennsylvania. During 1980–2 he was at the International Institute for Applied Systems Analysis (IIASA) in Laxemburg, Austria, as Task Leader of the Risk Group. His current research interests relate to decision-making for low probability events with an interest in the role of insurance and compensation as prescriptive tools. At IIASA he was involved in a multidisciplinary study of the decision processes associated with the siting of liquified energy gas (LEG) terminals in four different countries: the Federal Republic of Germany, the Netherlands, the United Kingdom and the United States. He is principal author of *Disaster Insurance Protection: Public Policy Lessons*.

Mark Pauly is Professor of Economics at Northwestern University. He has published work on insurance, health care and public finance, and is the author of *Doctors and their Workshops*. He is on the editorial boards of *Public Finance Quarterly, Inquiry* and the *Journal of Health Economics*. He is currently a research fellow at the International Institute of Management, Berlin.

W. Duncan Reekie obtained his PhD in Economics at the University of Strathclyde in 1969. He is a specialist in the economics of industrial organization and has held teaching posts in the University of the Witwatersrand, Johannesburg, and as Associate Professor in the University of Toronto. He now holds a Readership in Business Economics in the University of Edinburgh and was recently Visiting Professor, Pace University, New York. His books include *Advertising, The Economics of the Pharmaceutical Industry, Managerial Economics,*

Give Us This Day, Macroeconomics for Managers and *The Economics of Advertising*. He has contributed to professional periodicals, including *The Economic Journal, The Scottish Journal of Political Economy, Applied Economics*, and *The Journal of Industrial Economics*. He is also the editor of *Managerial and Decision Economics*.

Horst-Manfred Schellhaass is Professor of Economics at the Technical University of Berlin. His research is in the fields of competition theory and economic regulation with special interests in price regulations of the transportation and pharmaceutical industry and the regulatory practices in labour markets.

David S. Sibley is a member of the Economic Research Center at Bell Laboratories. He has also served at the US Civil Aeronautics Board and as a senior staff member at the Council of Economic Advisors in the Executive Office of the President. His research is in applied microeconomics, focusing on industrial organization and regulation. He is the author of numerous journal articles and is currently completing a book (with Stephen J. Brown) on public utility pricing.

Ulrich Stumpf is Assistant at the Technical University of Berlin. His research is in the fields of industrial organization and economic regulation, focusing on drug markets.

Robert D. Willig is Professor of Economics and Public Affairs at Princeton University. He previously supervised economic research at Bell Laboratories. He has written numerous articles on industrial organization, regulation and normative microeconomics, as well as *Welfare Analysis of Policies Affecting Prices and Products* and *Contestable Markets and the Theory of Industry Structure* (with W. Baumol and J. Panzar). He is a Fellow of the Econometric Society, a member of the editorial board of the *American Economic Review* and a consultant to government and industry on antitrust and regulation. He has testified before Federal Courts, regulatory agencies and the US Congress.

Part I
Introduction

1 Markets and Regulatory Policy in International Perspective

JÖRG FINSINGER

Few markets have escaped regulatory intervention by state authorities. State regulations almost everywhere guide and constrain market forces. The political process over-rides the market process to an extent which is incompatible with the spirit of a free market society. This view is held by a growing number of voters in many western countries. In the United States and in Great Britain government is actively engaged in reducing bureaucratic control in favour of more private initiative. In other countries, for example in the Federal Republic of Germany and some northern European countries, the continual growth of state intervention of the 1960s and 1970s has come to a halt. Increasingly, state intervention has been criticized for failing to achieve its objectives, or at least for failing to balance costs and benefits. Also, the need to avoid ever-increasing budget deficits in low-growth economies requires a careful reconsideration of government spending. However, deregulation policies have been tentatively adopted by only a few European industries – for example, bus transport and garbage disposal. The political process once more reveals its natural tendency to conserve the *status quo* and its property-right structure when there are conflicts of interest. There are other shortcomings of collective decision-making such as the tendency to ignore the long-run consequences of a change in the incentives for private agents. Thus, it seems that more thorough analysis of regulatory policies is urgently needed. The regulation conference and workshop held at Berlin in July 1981 were conceived to promote such studies. This book presents a selection of papers focusing on three major topics:

3

deregulation policies;
competition and regulation in insurance markets;
regulatory policies in pharmaceutical markets.

Chapter 2 in this volume, by William J. Baumol and Robert D. Willig,
applies the theory of natural monopoly and contestable markets to the
special case of railroad carriers. They argue that railroad carriers should
earn a rate of return equal to their cost of capital. The achievement of
financial viability is often prevented by certain rate calculation
principles – for instance, rate regulations based upon fully distributed
costs. Such price setting rules may not only lead to deficits, but may
ultimately be responsible for service deterioration and cumulative
abandonment of service. By contrast, the authors demonstrate that
there are sound pricing principles which remove the impediments to
adequate returns. These principles require demand-differentiated prices
which apportion common costs on the basis of value of service to
consumers. These demand-differentiated prices not only give the rail
carrier a maximal opportunity to cover cost, but also lead to an efficient
provision of rail service. This message should certainly be of great
interest in the US as well as in Europe, where railroads suffer from
chronic deficits. Moreover, it is demonstrated that these pricing
principles are not in conflict with deregulation policies. On the contrary,
market forces lead to the very same demand-differentiated prices.
Whenever a particular service is subject to competition, regulatory
intervention is not needed. When there is no competition and when
revenues fall short of costs, the most efficient use of transportation
services is promoted by those prices which maximize net revenues.
Again, no rate regulation is needed. Only when there is no competition
and when the carrier earns more than adequate returns on the invested
capital may rate ceilings be appropriate. Rate ceilings should not be
derived from fully distributed costs. There is only one appropriate
principle for determining rate ceilings which is based entirely on costs;
the stand-alone cost test. This requires that revenues from any service, or
group of services, be no greater than the cost of providing that service
on a stand-alone basis.

   Baumol's and Willig's arguments in favour of rate deregulation are
based on the recently developed theory of contestable markets. In this
theory it is not large numbers and price-taking behaviour which lead to
an optimal resource allocation. Rather, it is free entry and exit, that is,
the absence of entry barriers, which enforces socially optimal behaviour.
The threat of entry disciplines firms even when the market sustains only

a small number and when minimum efficient scale is large relative to the market. In particular, this power extends to natural monopolies which, in the past, were thought to require regulatory control. Of course, perfect contestability, total lack of entry barriers or no sunk costs related to entry, is likely to be satisfied by very few markets. For example, the railroad market is not perfectly contestable, but the 'invisible hand' is sufficiently strong to make rate regulation unnecessary whenever a service is threatened by entry or by intermodal competition. In contrast, US aviation markets come close to the ideal of a contestable market. For the capital to serve a particular city-pair market, aircraft can, literally, be flown in.

The degree of contestability of aviation markets is examined by Elizabeth E. Bailey, Daniel P. Kaplan and David S. Sibley. Until 1978, when the Airline Deregulation Act was passed, the Civil Aeronautics Board severely restricted entry into these markets. Thus, it was regulation which prevented contestability. The deregulation policy administered by the Civil Aeronautics Board basically consisted in the removal of licensing-related entry barriers. This deregulation policy, however, could only succeed in creating a contestable market, and thus promote economic efficiency, if there were no other entry barriers. If other important entry barriers existed, then concentration would persist; highly concentrated markets would remain highly concentrated. Bailey, Kaplan and Sibley find that this does not occur. With few exceptions, deregulation resulted in rapid deconcentration. They conclude that entry barriers are low at the hub and city-pair level. Some remaining entry barriers seem to be related to access restrictions to airports. Bailey, Kaplan and Sibley also examine the trends in fare structure. Deregulation has resulted in efficient fares responding better to cost and other market conditions than under regulation. However, they find that carriers in concentrated markets still have some price-setting power and, thus, full contestability has not yet been achieved.

There are other examples of markets, where natural barriers to entry and exit are low or non-existent, but where such barriers are created by regulatory policies. Solvency regulations, in particular minimal capital requirements, raise artificial entry barriers in most insurance markets. Government intervention often extends far beyond solvency regulations, mostly in order to prevent hypothesized market failure due to economies of scale or lack of consumer information. However, it is now clear that the existence of economies of scale is not a sufficient reason for regulatory control. In addition, most empirical studies suggest that there are no significant scale economies in the production of insurance. If scale economies must be discarded as a basis for justifying insurance regulation, there are still, undoubtedly, information imperfections which, as is often argued, are more serious than in other markets. It is well known that markets with incomplete or asymmetric distribution of information may fail to allocate resources efficiently. In particular, whenever lack of information leads to self-selection mechanisms, Cournot–Nash market equilibrium may not exist. When market equilibrium exists, it does not in general lead to an optimal allocation of resources. Markets with such deficiencies tend to be regulated. The insurance market provides a perfect example of a market with incomplete information and it is the focus of attention in Part III of this volume. Paul R. Kleindorfer and Howard Kunreuther demonstrate that the existence as well as the efficiency of insurance markets depend on consumer misperceptions of the risks that are being insured against.

In the framework analysed by Kleindorfer and Kunreuther, information on the probability of loss of different consumer classes is implicit in their choice of a particular insurance policy. However, firms do not try to learn about the risk of consumers from their actual loss experience. This learning process is the theme of Howard Kunreuther's and Mark Pauly's chapter. Firms update individual premiums in a Bayesian fashion using loss experience data. Consider a low-risk customer whose premium is adjusted downward over time, because he makes few claims. As long as his previous loss record is only available at his current insurance company, this firm has a certain monopoly power even if entry by new firms is costless and customers are free to leave their existing firms at will. The firm can charge each insured individual a higher premium than an actuarially fair experience rating based on his loss record. Kunreuther and Pauly argue that in this situation there are potential welfare gains from regulation. By forcing firms to disclose personal information on their customer's loss experience, insured individuals become better off. It is interesting to note that Germany has a mandated experience-rating scheme applying uniformly to all firms with required transfer of classification data between firms. Austria has recently adopted the same system.

The subsequent chapter, by Jörg Finsinger, studies actual insurance market performance in Germany. His main conclusions are as follows.

(1) The main purpose of the government interference in German insurance markets has been to prevent bankruptcy and to establish market transparency. Bankruptcy has been prevented, but market transparency is low. Certain regulatory policies ultimately cause intransparency.

(2) The lack of market transparency reduces competitive pressure. This is why, to an extent, differences in firm performance incompatible with a workably competitive market may persist.

(3) The regulation of profits and premiums leads to substantial input factor distortion. As a consequence, firms do not produce at minimum cost.

(4) Public enterprises and mutual companies outperform stock companies. One explanation for this performance difference is that the managements of firms with different ownership structures behave differently because they have different objectives. Regulatory constraints, consequently, have different impacts on firm behaviour. Take, for instance, public enterprises which, by their very constitution, do not make profits in the long run. All profits are paid back to the insured through dividends and rebates. Clearly, a regulatory constraint on profits is not binding for such a firm.

Conclusion (4) is at variance with findings of similar studies in the US, Canada and Great Britain. Since statistical analysis of additional data from German insurance companies[1] confirms conclusion (4), the question must be raised why ownership matters in Germany and not in other countries. Finsinger's paper suggests one possible answer; there is more price competition in insurance markets outside of Germany, where regulatory intervention makes real premiums uncertain by mandating complex dividend and rebate schemes.

Regulation of premiums and profits are thus shown to have adverse effects on overall market performance and, therefore, deregulation seems to be appropriate. However, there is one particular German insurance market where more regulatory action is required; this is the market for law-suit insurance. Law-suit insurance gives the policy holder the option to sue, free of any legal costs. The insurance pays for all lawyer fees as well as court costs. In Chapter 7 Michael Adams convincingly argues that such a full coverage insurance ultimately makes everybody worse off. He first constructs a model of the decision as to whether to go to court or to settle out of court. He then shows that a decrease in the cost of a law suit increases the number of disagreements actually taken to court. Besides presenting a novel approach to the economics of law, a number of policy relevant conclusions emerge.

(1) Any factors affecting legal costs or the subjective expectations of the parties at the same time affects the parties material rights.

(2) The insured parties gain at the expense of those who are not insured. This results in a redistribution of rights.

(3) Law-suit insurance leads to excessive numbers of law-suits and to high insurance premiums.
(4) Government should prevent companies who offer law insurance from undermining material rights by making a co-insurance clause mandatory which requires the parties in a law-suit to bear at least a fair fraction of the costs they impose.

While insurance markets are regulated in virtually all countries, pharmaceutical markets are heavily regulated in some countries – France, Italy, Belgium, Luxemburg, Greece, Ireland – but much less in others – Federal Republic of Germany, the Netherlands, Denmark, USA. These differences in regulatory policy between countries create their own problems, for most companies are multinational. In Part IV of this volume, Horst-Manfred Schellhaass and Ulrich Stumpf argue that national price and profit regulation may provide consumer benefits at the expense of customers in non-regulating countries. Such a 'beggar-my-neighbour' policy reduces the regulating country's share of common research and development costs. However, in the long run the rate of innovation is slowed down. Schellhaass and Stumpf describe the European drug regulation policies and examine the resulting price differentials. They find strong evidence that German consumers pay the highest drug prices and, thereby, finance the research and development ultimately benefiting other Common Market consumers. They conclude by calling for international agreements which prohibit such free riding.

In the final chapter W. Duncan Reekie takes up the issue of price comparisons which are often used in the pharmaceutical industry. All such studies in the past have been restricted to either individual products, single nation comparisons with other national markets, or identical drugs in a range of markets, even if the drugs were economically unimportant. His paper examines a large sample of analogous and important drugs from the USA, Europe and Japan. The sensitivity of the results to differing measures of 'price' is gauged, and the problem of fluctuating exchange rates is examined.

NOTES AND REFERENCES

1. Jörg Finsinger, 'Wettbewerb in Markt für Lebensversicherungen', *Zeitschrift für Betriebswirtschaft*, vol. 52, no. 2 (1982), p. 186.

Part II
Deregulation

2 Pricing Issues in the Deregulation of Railroad Rates

WILLIAM J. BAUMOL
and ROBERT D. WILLIG

INTRODUCTION

This chapter is addressed to the central pricing issues involved in partial deregulation of railroad rates. It enunciates principles to guide regulatory oversight of the rate setting of unsubsidized railroads – principles that are consistent with economic analysis and that are essential for protection of the public interest. The paper is largely motivated by the Staggers Rail Act, recently passed by the Congress of the United States, which mandates both an end to periodic Federal subsidies to railroads and continuing regulatory oversight of railroad rates. Nevertheless, the principles espoused here are equally germane wherever partial deregulation of railroads, or other utilities, is at issue.

In a regime of deregulation without general subsidies, one of the key elements in protecting the public interest is the avoidance of any residual regulation which effectively prevents the achievement of financial viability by the rail network. The public will hardly be well served by a set of regulatory rules which condemn the railroads to an inability to compete in the financial marketplace and which, consequently, will result in a rail network which is increasingly obsolete, is characterized by deterioration, and in which cumulative abandonment of service becomes the guiding principle.

In the following sections of this chapter we will discuss in detail the economically rational basis for the residual regulation of rates for rail transportation which will serve the public interest in a financially viable private sector rail system. This discussion begins with the fundamental principle that regulation should not impede railroads from earning a rate of return equal to their cost of capital, that is, a rate of return equal to that earned in a typical industry elsewhere in the economy and in which risks are similar to those of the railroads. From this principle, we proceed on the premise that any regulation of rates should promote economic efficiency which, by definition, will afford the greatest net benefits not only to carriers but also to shippers and to the public at large.

We will show why a system of rate regulation based upon fully distributed (or 'fully allocated') costs, where costs are apportioned on any basis other than demand, is inappropriate because prices set by that method are highly unlikely to permit railroads to achieve an adequate rate of return. Moreover, such a method leads to serious inefficiency by discouraging innovation and by generating prices which are too high to attract competitive traffic, which severely restrict the amount of services delivered by railroads, and which thus produce still higher rates for the remaining traffic.

By contrast, we will demonstrate that there are sound principles which promote economic efficiency while simultaneously removing impediments to adequate returns for carriers, and that these principles can be used in assessing the reasonableness of those rates which are judged to require continued oversight by the regulatory agency. These principles lead to demand differentiated prices, which are sometimes referred to as Ramsey prices, which apportion all unattributable fixed and common costs of the railroad among its services on the basis of the values of those services to consumers, mathematically expressed as their elasticities of demand. By providing that each service is priced at a markup over marginal costs which is inversely related to the elasticity of demand for that service, economically efficient differential pricing combines cost and demand factors in an optimal manner. These principles result in lower prices for shippers generally by establishing a set of rates which encourages the purchase of more transportation services by more shippers than artificial fully distributed cost based pricing, thereby creating a larger traffic base over which unattributable costs can be apportioned. They maximize the opportunity for rail carriers to earn an adequate return on capital, and they foster innovation and efficiency in the provision of rail transportation services by rewarding carriers who achieve cost reductions. Thus, net benefits to all consumers are maximized while the public's interest in a viable rail system is served.

As we shall show, economically efficient differential pricing is entirely consistent with the hallmark of deregulation: that market forces, rather than regulation, should control rates for transportation services. Thus, when a particular type of traffic is subject to competition, direct or indirect, regulatory intervention is unjustified because that competition will produce efficient prices without regulatory guidance. Furthermore, so long as an individual railroad's earnings fall short of its cost of capital, the need for regulatory constraints upon any of that carrier's rates is minimal and, to the extent such a constraint prevents the carrier from earning an adequate return in the future, it is contrary to the public interest. By definition, there is no danger that such a carrier is receiving excessive overall profits derived from market power or any other cause. In addition, if the rate for any service supplied by a railroad not yet earning adequate revenues overall is held down by regulation below that level which consumers of that service are prepared to pay rather than do without the service, then, in the long run, even those consumers will be harmed as the carrier finds it unprofitable to invest the necessary replacement and maintenance capital, causing a deterioration in, and ultimate withdrawal of, the service. Hence, for a railroad whose net revenues fall short of its cost of capital, the prices which promote the most efficient use of transportation services are those that maximize net revenues on each service.

We will also discuss the only economically defensible principle for determining a ceiling on rates for non-competitive traffic which is entirely based on costs. This is the stand-alone cost test, which establishes the basis for determining if the rate for a particular service is providing a true cross-subsidy to other services of the railroad.

In short, this chapter will describe a workable set of principles for the residual regulation of railroad rates appropriate for an era of deregulation. It will show why these principles constitute the package that most effectively serves the public interest. It will also show why regulation by fully distributed costs, which in the past has been a prime contributor to inefficiency and deterioration of the rail network, if re-adopted as a guide for the setting of ceilings upon rates will serve the economy in the future no better than it did in the past.

PRICING AND THE PUBLIC-INTEREST PHILOSOPHY

Prices serve two different purposes in a free-market economy. One of them is recognized by everyone while the other is often overlooked by those who have not studied the workings of the economy analytically. The first function of prices is to determine the distribution of wealth.

Thus, increases in wages make workers richer and employers less well off. This obvious role of prices often obscures their second function which economists consider to be of at least comparable importance: their role in guiding the allocation of resources so that those resources are used most efficiently in the ways that most effectively serve the needs and desires of consumers.[1]

By demanding particular goods, consumers bid their prices to a level sufficient to attract the materials, labour, and capital inputs necessary for their production. If prices do not reflect consumer preferences – if they are kept below the levels at which supplies are adequate to satisfy consumer demands – it means that insufficient quantities of inputs will be attracted to the production of these goods and services.

Firms are the conduit through which prices bring productive factors where they are needed to serve consumer demands. This holds for railroads just as it holds for any other industry. Thus, for rail services to be supplied on a continuing basis, in quantities and degrees of quality consistent with the desires of the consuming public, prices must be adequate to induce the firms, that is, the railroads, to acquire the necessary inputs, including the requisite capital.

Of course, this process is a two-way street. That is, while prices assure adaptation of the allocation of resources to the preferences of consumers, they also induce the adjustment of consumer demands to the available outputs and to the cost of providing them. The demand for fuels, for example, has fallen dramatically in the past few years and there can be little doubt that prices have played a substantial part in bringing this adjustment about.

Prices also guide investment decisions, influencing not only the overall magnitude of the accumulation of capital during a particular period, but also determining the apportionment of that capital among the different industries and their various economic activities.

In short, if prices are properly determined, they can prevent various types of economic waste. They can encourage increased consumption of those items whose resource cost has been reduced by innovation or by discovery of new sources or new materials, and discourage consumption of items which require large quantities of relatively scarce resources. They can assure the availability to each economic activity of the combination of inputs which keeps its relative costs to a minimum. They can assure the availability of capital and other inputs to productive activities whose outputs clearly justify their costs.

The economists' pricing philosophy is that where government intervenes in the process of price determination, it should always be done in a manner which serves the public interest by contributing as far as it can to the efficiency of resource allocation. That is, those prices should be chosen in such a way that their effects upon the allocation of inputs, upon the relative quantities of outputs demanded by consumers, and upon the formation of new capital that contributes to the economy's production capacity serve consumer needs and desires as effectively as possible. This, then, is the efficiency principle that guides our recommendations on price regulations.

One of the most crucial of the tasks that is assigned to prices is that they yield total revenues sufficiently large to cover production costs. This component of efficiency in pricing can perhaps be considered to be of over-riding importance, for if the requirement is violated for a particular service or set of services, in the long-run they will not be supplied. That is, the service for which compensatory pricing is somehow precluded must, sooner or later, disappear from the set of the economy's outputs, while in the short-run the product's quality and the efficiency with which it is produced can be expected to deteriorate. Private enterprise simply refuses to supply capital to activities which do not cover their costs. This is true even if these activities have benefits which exceed their costs, so long as interferences with the pricing process prevent prices from reflecting those benefits fully.

The roles of prices in allocating inputs, in adjusting demands and in apportioning new capital are also important, and are inextricably linked with one another. They are all part of the mechanism of consumers' sovereignty – the arrangement under which consumers, having decided, consciously or unconsciously, upon their preferences and priorities, can require the economy to respond by providing the appropriate goods and services in the appropriate quantities, and doing so as efficiently as possible. In this process it is the consumers who ultimately decide the uses to which capital assets will be put and it is prices which transmit the required information about consumer demands and enforce their satisfaction by suppliers.

Thus, the role of prices as a guide to the allocation of resources is essential to the health of the economy and to its effectiveness in serving the public interest. This, then, is the cornerstone of the economist's attitude toward pricing and toward the appropriateness of any regulatory activity that affects the selection of prices.

It should be emphasized again that under this philosophy there is an important sense in which the opportunity for financial viability for the supplier is the matter of highest priority. It is a condition absolutely necessary for the price mechanism to be able to carry out its other useful functions relating to the allocation of resources. For if there is no way in which the supplier can achieve financial viability, in the long-run he will have no choice but to abandon the supply activity involved. Supply of the good or service in question will first deteriorate and, ultimately, vanish so that neither efficiency in its supply nor rationality in its allocation will remain as pertinent issues.

The common sense philosophy which has just been described is what underlies the principles which are referred to as Ramsey pricing.[2] Ramsey prices are defined as those prices which induce the most efficient allocation of resources among all the sets of prices that are compatible with financial viability of the suppliers. That is, they are designed to make it possible for the firm's overall revenues to cover the total costs of the enterprise. But when a firm provides a variety of services, as when a railroad carries many different commodities over its various routes, there may be more than one set of prices that satisfies this financial viability requirement. If so, one can make up for lower prices on one service by higher prices on another. Ramsey prices then, are chosen from among the set of financially viable alternatives, and comprise that price for each particular movement or service which best meets the requirements of economic efficiency and, consequently, best serves the interests of consumers. These two elements, financial viability and economic efficiency, are the defining elements of any Ramsey pricing calculation.

THE PROPER CRITERION FOR ADEQUACY OF REVENUES

Since avoiding impairment of financial viability plays so crucial a role in any rational program of rate regulation, it is important to describe the criterion by which financial viability can be judged. Just what information is required to determine when a firm's revenues are adequate to cover its pertinent costs?

While the answer would appear to be obvious, the past history of regulation demonstrates rather forcefully that it is in fact widely misunderstood. The basic issue is that among the costs which must always be included in these calculations is the cost of the firm's capital, *including any capital it has generated internally.*

The logic of this criterion is straightforward. Revenues are defined to be adequate when they are just sufficient to enable the firm to attract the capital needed for maintenance, replacement, modernization and whatever expansion demand conditions justify. If revenues are lower than this, the deterioration and eventual disappearance of the service in question are a foregone conclusion.

The market for funds is one of the most competitive in the economy. It simply offers no room to those who cannot meet the competition for funds by others who come there to seek capital. If there are plenty of funds demanded by those who are willing and able to offer 18 per cent interest, then no funds will be available to a firm that can offer only 16 per cent and is about as risky as its rivals. Or rather, a firm that earns only 16 per cent can borrow for a while by mortgaging its future – by short-changing past investors in order to provide the new investors the 18 per cent return required by current market conditions. But no firm can continue to short-change past investors indefinitely, because the market soon learns how fragile its promises are. Thus, there is no escaping the following principles that determine the adequacy of revenues:

(1) The firm's overall rate of return must be equal to the returns currently earned by the typical firm with similar risks elsewhere in the economy. Otherwise the required funds will be denied to it.

(2) This means that adequacy of revenues can only be judged by comparison with earnings *outside* the regulated industry, not by comparing the regulated industry's earnings with the market value of its equity. For the market prices of those securities will automatically adjust themselves downward to match any act by the regulator which restricts the earnings of a firm below a compensatory rate of return, and so such a comparison will *appear* to justify any earnings restrictions, no matter how inappropriate.

(3) In determining the revenue requirements for financial viability, the rate of return obtained by comparison with other industries must be applied to a rate base which covers the economic replacement cost (under regulation) of all facilities. (Suitably updated historic costs may be utilized instead of replacement costs if the allowed rate is expressed in nominal terms.)

(4) With the rate base determined in this way and the rate of return on that rate base equal to the cost of capital, as given by earnings prevailing elsewhere in the economy, one will have determined the figure for total net earnings by the railroad that can appropriately be considered to be adequate for it to compete successfully in the capital market.

(5) This earnings figure must not be applied as a rigid ceiling. Otherwise railroads will not have the ability to earn this figure over the long run, since they will be precluded from making up for the revenue shortfalls which may occur as the result of temporary downward fluctuations in demand for their services.

Prices that make sense economically must *never be incompatible* with this earnings level. Of course, no prices can *guarantee* that a railroad will earn adequate returns overall. For if demands for its services are insufficient or the railroads' operations are conducted wastefully or its service is poor, even appropriate prices cannot be expected to lead to profitable operation. But once the railroads are permitted to charge appropriate prices, the regulatory impediments to financial viability will have been cleared away and it is then up to the railroads to take advantage of the opportunity by means of economy of operation, quality of service and effective marketing effort.

WHAT IS MEANT BY 'EFFICIENCY IN PRICING'?

Aside from the requirement that prices permit financial viability, what is meant by saying that one set of prices is 'more efficient' or that one set of prices is the *most* efficient of all the prices compatible with financial viability? As we discussed in the first section of this chapter, one of the principal roles that prices play in the economy is guidance of allocation of resources among their many possible uses. Economists judge the efficiency of prices in terms of the efficiency of the allocation of resources that they induce – that is, the extent to which resources are channelled by the prices into their best uses. Resources are utilized best when they yield the largest possible value to consumers, net of the costs of supplying them. Thus, the most efficient prices maximize the net benefits obtained by consumers.

Some simple examples may help to clarify this concept. Suppose some freight can be shipped between two points with equal speed and care by rail or by truck, either movement yielding the shipper a gross benefit of $1500. Suppose also that the costs incurred to move the freight by rail are $1000, while those for the truck movement are $1300. Let us consider the effects of prices for the rail and truck movements of $1400 and $1350, respectively. The shipper will respond to these prices by choosing the truck movement, because it is the cheaper one for him. The net benefit of this allocation is $1500 − $1300 = $200 – that is, the gross value to the shipper, net of the cost of supply. (Another equivalent view of this calculation is that the net benefit of $200 is equal to the surplus value to the shipper, over and above his payment for it, $1500 − $1350 = $150, plus the profit of the truck carrier, $1350 − $1300 = $50.) In contrast, consider the effects of alternative prices of $1300 and $1350 for the rail and truck movements respectively. These prices lead the shipper to choose the rail movement, and result in a higher net benefit of $1500 − $1000 = $500. Consequently, the prices of $1300 and $1350 are more efficient than the prices of $1400 and $1350. They induce a more efficient utilization of transportation resources.

It is instructive to see how, in this example, competition between unconstrained profit-oriented carriers results in efficient prices. Either firm would prefer to carry the freight at some price above its cost, rather than not carry it at all. Hence, the rail carrier will bid the price down to just below $1300, because the truck carrier cannot cover his cost at that price or less. The prices that result from competition, say $1299 and $1301 for rail and truck movements, are optimally efficient in that they yield the highest net benefits ($500) and guide the freight to move in the least costly way.

For another example, suppose that a coal shipper and a timber shipper would each like to move 1 million tons a year along a deteriorated 10 mile spur line whose rehabilitation and maintenance would cost $2 million a year. Suppose that the true variable costs (for fuel, labour, and car rental) amount to 10 cents per ton-mile for both the coal and timber movements, and that the gross benefits to their shippers are respectively 26 cents and 16 cents per ton-mile. Then, prices of 20 cents per ton-mile for both coal and timber might seem to be fair because they have the same variable costs and because 20 cents on each of the 20 million ton-miles would yield revenues of $4 million/year, just enough to cover both variable costs and the costs of the spur line. However, these prices are inefficient. They would result in an allocation of resources with zero net benefits because the timber would not move at all at a price of 20 cents/ton-mile; the coal movements alone could not provide revenues sufficient to cover the costs of the line; the rail carrier could not afford to rehabilitate the line; and so neither the coal nor the timber shipper would receive any benefits.

In contrast, the market oriented prices of 25 cents/ton-mile and 15 cents/ton-mile for coal and timber, respectively, *are* efficient. At these prices, both coal and timber can move along the line, the rail carrier can recover both its variable and its rehabilitation and maintenance costs, and the resulting net benefits are $200 000 a year. (Gross benefits each year are $4.2 million = $0.26 × 10 million + $0.16 million × 10 million. Annual costs of supply are $4 million = $2 million + $0.10 × 10 million + $0.10 × 10 million. The difference is the net benefit figure.) The coal and timber shippers share these net benefits equally, despite the disparity in the prices they are charged. As we shall discuss fully below, where common costs must be covered, it is market-oriented, demand-differentiated rates that are efficient and that do tend to distribute net benefits in an even-handed manner.

Economists have also shown that free competitive markets will automatically yield the prices that are efficient.[3] This is one of the prime characteristics of the workings of the invisible hand: that where it works well, that is, where suitable competitive pressures are present, no intervention is needed to assure adoption of the efficient prices. That is one of the reasons why, under deregulation, regulatory attention to prices in competitive markets is totally inappropriate. Market forces no doubt can perform far better than regulators or economists in determining what those prices should be.

But for those cases in which regulatory attention *is* required, economists have discovered criteria which help to determine which price for each particular service of a firm is efficient. One of these criteria merits review here before we turn to our analysis of fully distributed cost standards for pricing. This criterion is: in addition to providing adequate revenues, efficient prices must attract all customers who are willing to pay for a service an amount that exceeds its marginal (variable) cost. If a service has a value to consumers (as judged by the price they are willing to pay for it) which exceeds the cost of the resources needed to produce it, the supply of that service is justified in terms of its social benefits, as long as its provision does not impede financial viability. Consequently, any price which precludes provision and sale of that service must be inefficient unless it is necessary for revenue adequacy.

As we explain more fully below in the section concerning Ramsey pricing for rail carriers with adequate revenues, in this criterion marginal costs must be calculated in terms of the value of the required resources in alternative uses (economists refer to these as 'opportunity costs'). Thus, cars and locomotives must be evaluated at their full capital costs as long as there are alternative uses for them anywhere. To this, of course, must be added the obvious variable costs, such as necessary labour, fuel and traffic-sensitive maintenance costs, since together those are the true variable costs of the traffic in question.

FULLY DISTRIBUTED COSTS AS IMPEDIMENTS TO EFFICIENT PRICING

There is a long tradition among regulatory agencies of reliance upon fully distributed costs in the determination of prices. For the most part, fully distributed costs have been used in the determination of floors under particular prices when that was considered a proper object of regulatory attention. But now, with deregulation, the imposition of rate floors that are above variable costs is recognized to be counterproductive and, instead, attention has shifted to the determination of ceilings for the prices of particular services. Curiously, the fully distributed cost criterion has re-emerged as a candidate for that job as well. From the economists' point of view this is ironic, for having recognized its destructiveness and inefficiency in the process of rate-floor determination, it would seem that regulators would have accepted at least the presumption that it is also counterproductive in the calculation of ceilings. One is driven to the suspicion that (apparent) ease of calculation threatens to become an over-riding consideration taking precedence over any consequences for social welfare and economic efficiency.

In any event, the shortcomings of fully distributed cost as a criterion for rate ceilings need not be inferred merely by presumption. As we will now show, fully distributed cost ceilings fail badly on both the counts we have been emphasizing: they can effectively preclude the earning of adequate revenues by a regulated railroad and they undermine any hope for the achievement of efficient utilization of transportation resources.[4] Rate ceilings based on fully distributed costs will typically lead to the provision of less service, higher prices, less benefits to shippers, less innovation, less competition, and fewer long-term contracts between shippers and railroads.

A simple example can most clearly demonstrate some of the ill effects of fully distributed cost rate ceilings. Consider a railroad with total unattributable costs of $360 million, and two types of potential traffic, *A* and *B*. In the absence of any regulation, suppose that service *A* would be able to provide $300 million of revenues above its attributable cost, and service *B* would be able to contribute $100 million above its attributable cost. These figures reflect the value of rail service to the shippers involved. Let us suppose that traffic *A* and *B* entail equal quantities of ton-miles and tons of shipments. Then, if all traffic moved, the fully distributed cost rate ceiling would constrain the net revenues earned on service *A* to be $180 million (one-half of the unattributable costs of $360 million), and the same for service *B*. While the railroad could obtain $180 million in net revenues from service *A*, it could only earn $100 million from service *B*. Thus, with fully distributed cost rate ceilings, by providing both services *A* and *B* the railroad could earn a maximum of only $280 million toward its unattributable costs of $360 million.

However, by pricing service *B* out of the market via rates set at the fully distributed cost ceiling, the railroad could shrink its traffic base and thereby raise the fully distributed cost ceiling for service *A* to the point where it could then gain net revenues of $300 million from that service. Despite the fact that service *B* could more than cover its own costs, by dropping it the railroad could raise its total net revenues from $280 to $300 million. Here, it should also be noted that because of the fully distributed cost rate ceilings, the most the railroad can earn is $300 million in net revenues, which is inadequate in view of its $360 million in unattributable costs.

In contrast, in the absence of fully distributed cost rate ceilings, the railroad could set its rates so that traffic *A* moves and provides a contribution of $270 million, and so that traffic *B* moves and provides a contribution of $90 million. It is essential to note that these market-determined rates provide adequate net revenues of $360 million, while no rates under fully distributed cost ceilings can provide adequate revenues. The market-determined rates move both traffic *A* and *B*, while the best rates for the railroad under fully distributed cost ceilings move only traffic *A*. The latter require the shippers of traffic *A* to contribute $300 million above their attributable costs, while the former require only $270 million from them. The latter leave the shippers of traffic *A* with no benefits net of their payments, and make it impossible for the shippers of traffic *B* to utilize rail service at all. In sharp contrast, the market determined rates leave shippers of traffic *A* and *B* with $30 million and $10 million, respectively, in value from their rail services over and above their payments for them.[5]

While the deleterious consequences of fully distributed cost rate ceilings are most clearly illustrated by simple examples of this kind, they are equally likely in the complex reality of the railroad industry. The features of the preceding example that account for the social damage caused by fully distributed cost rate ceilings are (1) the substantial unattributable costs, and (2) the diversity in the values above attributable costs of different rail services to shippers – values that are proportional neither to the ton-miles, nor to the tons involved, nor to any combination of the two. It is clear that these features of the example are also features of the railroad industry. Substantial portions of railroad costs are common, fixed and unattributable to individual services. And rail services do yield diverse values that depend on the commodities shipped and on the origins and destinations of shipments, as well as on the tons and ton-miles involved.

It may seem paradoxical that fully allocated cost criteria, that are apparently designed to assure that *all* costs are covered by revenues, can in fact preclude rail carriers from earning enough for financial viability. The reason is that ceilings based on fully distributed costs are set so that unattributable costs are divided in an arbitrary manner among all types of traffic. Then, for the unattributable costs to be covered by net revenues, all types of traffic must actually move at the rates that include the arbitrary cost allocations. But traffic with a transport value that is below average for its tons and ton-miles will not move by rail at those rates. Consequently, if the unattributable costs are substantial, and if the values of rail services vary substantially, then fully distributed cost rate ceilings will preclude attainment of adequate revenues. In this sense, the adoption of fully distributed cost standards can dash the most basic hope for deregulation – that it would at last make it possible for the railroads to regain their financial health.

The effects of fully distributed cost pricing on the efficiency of the utilization of transport resources will be equally pernicious. In doing their best to earn adequate revenues despite the handicap imposed by fully distributed cost rate ceilings, rail carriers will be unable to preserve traffic whose value to the shipper exceeds its attributable cost, but which falls sufficiently far below fully allocated cost. True, in the absence of fully distributed cost regulation any such traffic could contribute revenues that exceed the costs that it causes and would provide social benefits greater than social costs. But with fully distributed cost rate ceilings, this traffic will reduce the net revenues of the rail carrier and will thus not be compensatory. The reason is that this traffic will be assigned its portion of unattributable costs on the basis of its tons and ton-miles, thereby reducing the share of those costs allocated to other traffic with higher value, and consequently reducing the ceiling and the rates on that traffic.

It can be demonstrated mathematically that with fully distributed cost rate ceilings the net revenues of a railroad will be diminished if it carries any freight at a positive mark-up above attributable cost that is less than a critical percentage of the fully distributed cost mark-up. This critical percentage is equal to the percentage of all the railroad's freight that it is able to price at the fully distributed cost rate ceiling. In contrast, without fully distributed cost rate ceilings any unit of freight that can be carried at any positive mark-up above attributable cost will increase net revenues. Thus, with fully distributed cost rate ceilings, a railroad attempting to reach adequate revenues must price so as to suppress traffic that is capable of making a positive contribution, but whose contribution is below the critical percentage of the fully distributed cost mark-up. And the critical percentage is higher, and thus excludes more traffic, the more of the rail carrier's freight is priced at the ceiling. Yet, to approach adequacy of revenues, the railroad must price nearly all its traffic at the fully distributed cost ceiling.

The conclusions of this analysis are extremely disquieting. Under a system of fully distributed cost rate ceilings, because they must seek adequate revenues, railroads cannot afford to carry freight which is unable to bear rates close to the ceiling. Thus, too little traffic will move by rail. Further, the loss of contribution to unattributable costs from the suppressed traffic means that the rates on the traffic that is carried must be correspondingly higher if it is to cover total costs. Moreover, because the suppressed traffic could have generated benefits to shippers that exceeded the costs that they caused, the net benefits derived from the transport system are diminished. These effects can all be very substantial and will cause substantial injury to shippers and rail carriers alike if a substantial portion of current traffic will move at rates above the fully distributed cost ceiling, while another substantial portion of current and potential traffic will move only at rates between attributable costs and the fully distributed cost ceiling.

Fully distributed cost rate ceilings will also stifle the increases in railroad innovativeness and competitiveness that would otherwise be among the achievements of deregulation. A rail carrier cannot be expected to invest in new facilities, in research and development, and in marketing activities designed to develop new traffic if the financial gains from the new traffic are counterbalanced by induced decreases in the ceilings on the rates charged for pre-existing traffic. Similarly, a rail carrier cannot be expected to compete for freight by offering low rates if the necessary mark-ups are much below the arbitrary allocations of unattributable costs. However, in the absence of fully distributed cost rate ceilings, under deregulation railroads will have powerful new incentives to invest and compete for new traffic, even if that traffic at first yields a contribution to unattributable cost which is below average, but is nevertheless positive.

Finally, fully distributed cost rate ceilings will impede the beneficial trend toward the adoption of long-term contracts between railroads and shippers. Such contracts can greatly enhance the efficiency with which transport resources are utilized, by facilitating the planning of both rail carriers and shippers, by encouraging investments in committed resources needed to provide rail services, and by permitting adequate compensation for all rail shipments whose value is above marginal cost. Because the social efficiency gains from long-term contracts yield corresponding financial gains to both railroads and shippers, free market pricing can confidently be expected to stimulate significant numbers of contract rates. However, under fully distributed cost pricing, railroads will find it impossible to enter long-term contracts for any new traffic unless it can pay not only for itself but also for the reduction in rates on old traffic caused by the resulting decreases in fully distributed cost ceilings. Moreover, the flexibility in market pricing that contract rates make possible is lost when mechanistic pricing and rate-ceilings based on fully distributed cost are the rule.

The ultimate reason for these conclusions is that any artificial constraint such as the requirement of uniformity in the ratio between price and variable cost or tons/ton-miles (which is the implicit premise in the philosophy of fully distributed cost pricing) unnecessarily hamstrings industry and its management in its quest for ways to improve its business and to serve its customers most effectively.

RAMSEY PRICING BEFORE RAILROADS ACHIEVE ADEQUATE REVENUES

There is good reason to believe that with effective deregulation US railroads will, within the foreseeable future, be able to achieve adequate revenues, that is, rates of return equal to their cost of capital. But this cannot be expected overnight, and the pricing rules that are employed in the interim can significantly affect the speed and probability of the attainment of adequate revenues. Ill-advised residual rate regulations can impede, delay and even preclude attainment of this objective. For this reason it is important to consider carefully the appropriate regulatory rules for the interim period when adequacy of revenues has not yet been achieved.

As we discussed in the first section of this chapter, Ramsey prices are those which induce the most efficient allocation of resources, among the sets of prices that are compatible with the financial viability of the supplier. The rules of Ramsey pricing have been described extensively by economists for the case in which adequate revenues for the firm are in fact currently attainable. But less has been written about the case where this is not yet possible, and so this issue requires discussion here.

In principle, the rule determining Ramsey prices in this case is straightforward. Ramsey prices are simply those that maximize the firm's net revenue, if its total revenue is not yet adequate. The logic of this principle is not difficult to explain. As has already been emphasized, adequacy of revenues is the fundamental and over-riding necessary condition for economic efficiency. For, in its absence no service will continue to be supplied by private enterprise, and inadequate maintenance and replacement can be expected to lead to immediate deterioration in service quality. In sum, in the absence of adequate revenues, no matter what relative prices are adopted, efficient service is hardly to be expected. So long as market demands do not absolutely preclude adequate revenues (as will be true where an industry becomes totally obsolete), it is appropriate to do anything which achieves adequate revenues as quickly as possible and which in the meantime approaches that state as closely as cost and market conditions permit.

But maximization of net revenues is not defensible merely as a means to approximate financial viability. It also entails decisions and behavior patterns on the part of the firm which will, in and of themselves, serve the public interest.

(1) When net-revenue-maximizing prices can be determined movement by movement and shipper by shipper, all prices will equal or exceed the corresponding marginal costs. Otherwise, the movement would be a drain on net revenues which the carrier would prefer to avoid, and could avoid by the simple expedient of raising the price. (The price increase would eliminate the drain either by eliminating the movement or by increasing its revenues.) Prices that equal or exceed marginal costs induce the movement of any and all traffic whose value to the shipper exceeds its price and, consequently, its marginal cost. We have already noted that this is a fundamental requirement of efficiency in pricing.

(2) The deviations between prices and marginal costs will be higher for traffic whose value to shippers is higher. More specifically, the mark-up of price above marginal cost will vary inversely with what economists call the elasticity of demand.[6] That is, traffic whose value to shippers is low, as indicated by a great shrinkage in demand when price is raised slightly, will have a relatively small percentage mark-up of price over marginal cost, and the reverse will be true of items with a large value of service to shippers as shown by a low elasticity of demand (a small propensity to contraction in quantity demanded in response to a rise in price).

It is both necessary and efficient for traffic with higher value to shippers to be assessed higher mark-ups. The mark-ups are needed because fixed and common unattributable costs must be defrayed, and because it is the higher value traffic that can move at the higher prices. If the unattributable costs remain uncovered, the system will deteriorate and ultimately no traffic will be able to move.

(3) The prices which maximize net revenues are guaranteed to avoid cross subsidies automatically. For any service which is priced in such a way as to be the beneficiary of a cross subsidy must necessarily eat into the firm's net revenues. That is, net revenues can always be increased either by adopting a new price for that service which eliminates the cross subsidy or, if that is not possible, by dropping the service altogether. In either case, elimination of the cross subsidy will constitute an addition to the firm's net revenue. Thus, under a regime of net revenue maximization, the problem of cross subsidies automatically takes care of itself.

(4) The prices that maximize net revenues must be adapted to competitive pressures. A rise in price will surely not contribute to net revenue if it simply causes the affected traffic to be lost to another firm. What is relevant here is not only intermodal competition, but also competition among railroads and competition among sources of the products shipped and any substitutable products. The value of the service to the shipper is, of course, affected by the cost of shipment via another mode or another railroad. Moreover, that value is affected by the cost to the recipient getting a similar commodity from another source. A coal burning utility will not pay a high price for coal from mine *A* which must be shipped via railroad *B* if that coal can be obtained more cheaply from mine *C* which ships via railroad *D*, and this effectively constrains the rates charged for coal transportation by railroad *B*. All this must be taken into account in the determination of net-revenue maximizing rates, and the railroads themselves are surely in the best position to do so.

(5) Any arbitrary constraint upon rates that is imposed by regulators, such as the requirement that the prices of certain types of traffic have a common mark-up over variable costs, must necessarily reduce the railroads' net revenues, and, in the period before adequate returns are achieved, this must necessarily damage further their ability to raise the capital they require, as well as contributing to inefficiency. The same must be true of any other inflexibilities imposed by regulation, such as delays in the process by which required rate changes are carried out.

(6) In all this nothing has yet been said about the inevitable concern that can be expected to be expressed about the setting of rates for the exceptional cases of traffic for which competition is absent – that is, traffic which faces no competition from other railroads, other modes

or other sources of supply. It is to be emphasized that for traffic which faces competition from any source, regulatory attention to rates is certainly unjustified, and must undermine the spirit and substance of deregulation. But for traffic for which competition of any kind is absent, it may be considered essential to place some upper bounds upon rates. An economically defensible criterion for this purpose, the stand-alone cost test, will be described presently in the section concerned with stand-alone cost as a rate ceiling. However, as is shown there, this test is logically equivalent to tests for cross-subsidization, and, as we have said above, maximization of net revenues precludes cross-subsidies.

(7) Finally, it should be emphasized that the management of a railroad without adequate revenues has strong incentives to set rates in the manner required for net revenue maximization, to the extent permitted by regulation. Without adequate revenues, the railroad cannot obtain the capital it needs for expansion, modernization and maintenance. Inadequate revenues depress the asset value of the enterprise and its long-run size. And all the statistical evidence confirms that managerial prestige and compensation are influenced most heavily by two variables: the firm's profits, and size. Both these influences, then, clearly put pressure on management to leave no stone unturned in seeking to increase company profits and to gain full access to the capital market.

There is at least one more reason why the managements of railroads with inadequate revenues will be forced to maximize profits. Once deregulation has occurred, railroads which fail to take full advantage of their profit opportunities will leave themselves open to attempted take-overs. True, this did not occur under regulation since the regulatory constraints left little scope for profit from the take-over process. But under deregulation, if management were lax in its pursuit of profit opportunities, the price of the railroad's stocks would normally be correspondingly low. That is, those stocks would then reflect what the railroad actually earns rather than the larger amount it is capable of earning, and that is exactly the sort of situation which invites take-overs.

In short, management will have much to gain by pursuing every available profit opportunity and, moreover, will not be given the chance to do otherwise. Thus the free market will provide the pressures to force management to adopt the pricing and output decisions consistent with profit maximization, particularly so long as revenues are inadequate.

And they will thereby be led to make the decisions which, as we have seen, the public interest requires.

Of course, even with the best of will and strongest of incentives, management cannot be expected to achieve more than an approximation to absolute maximization of net revenues. Market information is inevitably imperfect and costs and business conditions are always changing. Business decisions that best balance risks and best weigh imperfect information in advance will rarely appear best with the benefit of hindsight. But because they are closest to the market and have the most to gain, it is the firms themselves that are best equipped to make the most appropriate decisions concerning their own operations and pricing. Pursuit of the objective of net-revenue maximization is best left to the railroads' managements, without unnecessary intervention by regulators.

RAMSEY PRICING FOR RAIL CARRIERS WITH ADEQUATE REVENUES

The Inverse Elasticity Rule

As we have just discussed, for a rail carrier that is unable to achieve adequate revenues, the Ramsey prices, or public interest prices, are those that maximize net revenues. Similarly, these prices are also Ramsey optimal for a rail carrier that is just able to obtain adequate revenues via the rates that maximize net revenues, and that is unable to obtain adequate revenues with any other rates. The question we address in this section is what are the Ramsey, public interest prices for a rail carrier that is able to obtain adequate revenues from two or more different sets of rates.

We have seen that the overriding consideration here is the financial viability of the rail carrier. Thus, the public interest prices must earn net revenues that are sufficient to cover the cost of the capital employed by the carrier. And, among the sets of rates that yield adequate revenues, the prices chosen should be those that promote the most efficient use of transportation services and that are best for the totality of the consumers of the carrier's services. By definition, these are the Ramsey prices.

For reasons we shall explain below, the Ramsey prices provide mark-ups above marginal costs that are different for different services, and that depend on the demand characteristics of the services in a manner we shall describe. In total, these mark-ups yield net revenues that cover the fixed and common costs of the rail carrier that cannot be attributed to individual services. Hence, Ramsey prices may be interpreted to determine implicitly an allocation among services of the carrier's unattributable costs. This allocation depends upon the demand characteristics of the services, and is the one that is most efficient economically. As we explain below, it is also an equitable allocation and is feasible in practice. It should be emphasized that it is the Ramsey prices alone that will yield the best allocation of unattributable fixed and common costs – no other method of allocating these costs among services is consistent with economic efficiency. In particular, as was shown above in the section concerned with fully distributed costs as impediments to efficient pricing, *pro rata* or other arbitrary methods of allocation, no matter how appealing they may be superficially, are consistent only with prices that are distinctly less efficient in general than are Ramsey prices, and, moreover, they will generally fail to provide adequate revenues.

Ramsey prices lie above marginal costs and involve percentage mark-ups above those costs that are inversely proportional to price elasticities of demand. This relationship is generally recognized and is called the inverse elasticity rule.[7] It indicates that services whose demands are highly elastic should be assigned prices very close to their marginal costs, while services whose demands are very inelastic should be priced well above those costs. The magnitude of these mark-ups among all services must be sufficiently high to earn net revenues that cover fixed and common costs – that is, that achieve revenue adequacy. The amounts of the mark-ups over marginal costs for different services should be different, with the larger mark-ups earned on services with relatively inelastic demands.

Before discussing the logic of this result we may first define precisely what we mean by the terms 'elasticity of demand' and 'marginal cost'.

Demand Elasticity and Value of Service

The elasticity of demand provides a quantitative interpretation of the traditional concept, *value of service*, which has played so important a role in public utility pricing. Consumers who place relatively high value on a service will have demands for it that are relatively inelastic, and vice-versa. For if a rise in price would lead to no significant reduction in quantity demanded (that is, if demand is *inelastic*), then the service must be worth at least the higher price to its consumers, that is, the value of the service must be high. Conversely, if a rise in the price of a service would lead consumers to curtail their demand substantially (that is, if demand is quite elastic), then the service must be worth little or no more to its consumers than the original price, so that the value of the service must be low.

In view of this correspondence between value of service and demand elasticity, the inverse elasticity rule of Ramsey pricing can be restated in terms that may be more familiar. It should be the services with relatively high values to their consumers that contribute relatively large net revenues to the coverage of unattributable, fixed and common costs. Thus, the implicit allocation of unattributable costs should be based on value of service, rather than any *pro rata* sharing or other arbitrary method. This is a familiar and long-used principle in railroad pricing, but it is the Ramsey analysis which first provided rigorous underpinnings for its utilization. While the value of service characterization of Ramsey pricing is essentially accurate, the inverse elasticity rule ensures that the value-of-service data are used in a manner consistent with economic efficiency, and does so in a manner that provides explicit guidance for pricing. For example, one lesson of the inverse elasticity rule is that the relevant elasticity of demand is that facing the rail carrier whose prices are at issue. This concept is unambiguously defined to reflect the sensitivity of demand for the carrier's service to changes in the price set by the carrier for the service.

It is clear that all factors that influence a rail carrier's elasticities of demand are relevant for the carrier's Ramsey prices. These factors may include the value of the commodity shipped, intermodal competition, intramodal competition, source competition, interport competition, and the substitutability of other commodities for the one shipped at its destination. All of these factors, and others as well, shape the markets for transportation services in which a rail carrier operates, and together determine the elasticities of demand for its services. Any of these factors is more important than another for the determination of the Ramsey prices only to the extent that it has a more important influence on the carrier's market demands.

Hence, when we assert that unattributable costs should be apportioned on the basis of value of service, we mean by 'value of service' the value of the rail carrier's service in the relevant transportation market, with all demand factors considered. Value of service is thus properly construed as a market concept.[8]

Another important lesson of the inverse elasticity rule is that marginal cost is the cost datum with which it is appropriate to compare a rate for the purpose of Ramsey pricing.

The Definition of Marginal Cost

The marginal cost of a service is the additional cost that would be incurred in supplying an additional unit, or the saving in total cost that would be made possible by supplying one less unit. As such, the marginal cost of a rail service is the per-unit opportunity cost to the rail carrier of the resources employed to supply the last units of the service. Here the term 'opportunity cost' refers to the value a resource can contribute if it is used in some alternative occupation instead of the one to which it is currently assigned by the railroad. Thus, marginal cost is similar in meaning to unit incremental cost and to the true economic variable cost. However, the definition of marginal cost makes it clear that it should include the costs of capital facilities that are fungible and economically attributable to the service, as well as the more obvious cost components such as fuel, labour, and traffic-sensitive maintenance costs.

Of course, the marginal cost of a service also includes the wear-and-tear on capital assets and the required maintenance expenses that the supply of the service causes. The costs of facilities that are fixed or common are not included in a service's marginal costs, nor should they be allocated to it on bases such as usage, tons, or ton-miles. Instead, it should be recognized that no portion of these costs is attributable to any one of the services that utilize the facilities, and can legitimately be allocated only implicitly through the net revenues that the Ramsey prices generate.

The Logic of the Inverse Elasticity Rule – Efficiency and Equity

As we have said, for a carrier with adequate revenues the Ramsey prices are defined to be those prices (among all possible sets of prices that generate adequate revenues) that induce the most efficient utilization of transportation services. And a widely known mathematical result is that the Ramsey prices, so defined, satisfy the inverse elasticity rule.[9]

It is easy to explain why Ramsey prices are equitable. First, they are non-discriminatory in the sense that services with similar economic characteristics will have similar Ramsey prices, whatever the commodities shipped, whatever the route and whatever the identity of the shipper. That is, two different services with the same elasticities of demand will be priced at the same percentage mark-ups above marginal costs. And, two different services with the same marginal costs and with the same demand elasticities will bear identical Ramsey prices.

Second, under Ramsey pricing, consumers of the rail carrier's services who obtain services with a higher value to them bear more of the unattributable fixed and common costs. These costs are necessary for the supply of all of the carrier's services, and it is certainly not inequitable for those who value the supply of those services more highly to bear a greater portion of those requisite costs. In fact, as will become clear from our discussion of their efficiency, the Ramsey prices allocate the unattributable rail carrier costs among the various services in such a manner that the payment by consumers of each service is roughly proportional to the values of the service. Thus, while the Ramsey prices of different services are different proportions of the services' marginal costs, the burdens from these necessary mark-ups that are borne by the consumers of different services have roughly the same proportion to their respective values of service.

It should be emphasized here that since it is only the firm's necessary costs, including the cost of capital, that are covered by Ramsey prices, Ramsey pricing is not equivalent to 'charging what the traffic will bear'.[10] Rather, Ramsey prices are lower, overall, than those that the traffic would bear, provided that the rail carrier could, if unconstrained by regulation, earn a rate of return on its capital in excess of its cost of capital. On the other hand, if 'all that the traffic will bear' is just the cost of carrying that traffic, then, of course, that is what efficiency and equity dictate that the traffic should pay.

We come, finally, to the efficiency grounds that underlie the inverse elasticity rule of Ramsey pricing. Economists have been concerned primarily with this efficiency argument and it is the prime reason for our acceptance of Ramsey pricing. Thus, although the logic of this argument is unfortunately more complicated than that of the equity argument, it is nevertheless important to recount it here.

If there were no need for enterprises to be financially self-supporting, an ideally efficient allocation of society's resources would be brought about if the price of each good or service were equal to its marginal cost. At such prices, consumers elect to purchase all units of goods and services that yield them benefits larger than the costs of providing them. And, in response to such prices, consumers avoid purchasing units that yield them benefits smaller than the costs of providing them. As a result, the economy misses no opportunity to allocate resources to uses where they yield benefits greater than costs, and no resources are allocated to uses with benefits lower than costs. Consequently, the allocation that is brought about by prices equal to marginal costs yields the greatest obtainable total net benefit, and is ideally efficient.

However, prices equal to marginal costs would provide revenues insufficient to cover a rail carrier's fixed and common costs, and would make it impossible for the supply of rail services to become financially self-supporting. Thus, the Ramsey prices are those that do make possible financially self-supporting firms and that distort as little as possible the ideally efficient allocation of resources. In the language of technical economics, the Ramsey prices maximize the consumers' surplus from the carrier's services, subject to a revenue adequacy constraint.

The Ramsey prices induce all groups of consumers to reduce their consumption in roughly equal proportions below the ideal or optimal quantities.[11] They cause roughly equiproportional decreases in the level of consumers' surplus derived from each service, relative to that enjoyed at prices equal to marginal costs. They generate net revenues from each service that are less by roughly equal proportions than those that are the largest possible under the conditions of the market.[12]

For prices to lead to the optimal equal percentage reductions in quantities demanded from their ideal levels, it is necessary that the prices themselves depart unequally from the corresponding marginal costs. For example, if all prices were set above marginal costs by the same percentage mark-up, the purchase of services with larger elasticities of demand would be cut further from their ideal levels than the purchases of those services with smaller elasticities of demand. The balanced changes in quantities that maximize the total net benefits of consumers are achieved by prices that obey the inverse elasticity rule. For, then, the greater ratios of price to marginal cost are assigned to those services whose demands are more resistant to distortion, that is, to those with relatively small elasticity of demand.

Increases above marginal cost in the price of an elastic service causes much traffic to be lost – traffic that would generate net benefits because it is valued above the cost that it causes. However, less traffic is lost when the price of an inelastic service is raised, and the traffic that is curtailed is the least valued portion. Consequently, when prices must be elevated above marginal costs to cover unattributable costs, it is economically efficient to increase prices of inelastic services more than prices of elastic ones. Such Ramsey prices are, on average, the lowest consistent with financial viability. They result in more traffic, more net benefits to the totality of shippers, and more net benefits to society.

To make clear the benefits offered by Ramsey pricing, let us suppose that a carrier with adequate revenues has violated the Ramsey rule by levying equal mark-ups (greater than $1 in this example) on an inelastic and an elastic service with equal numbers of units of traffic. Let us see how matters can be improved. An increase of $ 1 in the rate on the highly inelastic service must, of course, yield the carrier additional net revenues equal to $1 on each unit of traffic, while a decrease of $1 in the rate on the elastic service must diminish the carrier's net revenues by $1 on each original unit of traffic. But there will be important offsetting effects. Because the latter service has an elastic demand, shippers will respond to the $1 rate decrease by expanding traffic. The new traffic will yield new positive net revenues that offset the revenue loss. Thus, the increase in net revenue from a rise in the price of an inelastic service is greater than the loss in net revenue from a reduction in the price of an elastic service. Consequently, the carrier can reduce the rate on the elastic service by $1 and yet continue to earn adequate revenues. This step toward market pricing permits adequate revenues to be obtained from prices that are lower, on average.

Moreover, while the rate increase on the inelastic service does not suppress much, if any, traffic, the rate decrease on the elastic service stimulates much new traffic whose value exceeds the cost that it causes. This expansion of rail traffic constitutes an increase in the efficiency of utilization of transportation resources. It generates benefits to the shippers that exceed the rate decrease on their original traffic flows and that therefore considerably exceed the costs of the rate increase borne by the users of the inelastic service. The expansion of rail traffic represents an increase in the flow of commodities to their markets at lower transportation costs. As a result, social productivity is enhanced, and more consumers can obtain more of the goods they desire at lower costs of supply.

The Imposition of Constraints on Prices Beyond the Requirement of Revenue Adequacy Diminishes Efficiency

The Ramsey analysis indicates that the most efficient utilization of society's transportation resources results from Ramsey prices and that these prices differ whenever marginal costs and elasticities of demand differ. Hence, efficiency and the preferences of consumers as a group are best served by a rate structure for rail services that is sufficiently flexible to accommodate price differences wherever there are differences in either costs or in demand characteristics.

Of course, practicality requires uniformity of rates for services or movements that are indistinguishable from one another to the carrier, or that can only be distinguished by obtaining information at costs that exceed their benefits. Such a limited degree of uniformity in rates is justifiable only by either inevitabilities or efficiency considerations relating to information costs. In addition, Ramsey prices will be uniform for services whose marginal costs and demand elasticities are similar.

However, uniformity of prices or of ratios of prices to marginal costs that is imposed by regulatory constraint results in total net benefits to consumers from transportation services that are smaller than those available from Ramsey prices constrained only by the requirement that revenues be adequate. In fact, it can be demonstrated mathematically that the most efficient prices yielding revenues that are possible under imposed uniformity constraints have higher average ratios to marginal costs than the true Ramsey prices that yield adequate revenues.

This reasoning applies with equal force to movements of different sizes and to shippers who move different quantities per year. That is, efficient prices will be differentiated on the basis of the quantity shipped, to the extent that either marginal costs or demand elasticities also vary on that basis.[13] Hence, constraints that prevent such pricing must reduce net benefits to consumers.

Ramsey Pricing for Competitive Services

In the economics literature, Ramsey prices are usually defined and analyzed for a natural monopoly enterprise which faces no competition for its products and services. However, here we have followed the writings of some other economists,[14] as well as our own[15] in applying the same philosophy of Ramsey pricing to an enterprise like a rail carrier which is active in a wide variety of markets involving varying degrees and kinds of competition. Only one proviso is required to explain this generalization of the more usual analysis. Here, we have analyzed the prices of a given rail carrier that are most efficient among those that yield adequate revenues, taking as given the pricing and other market behavior of any other suppliers of competing transportation services. This frame of reference is that which is most appropriate for the analysis of the pricing of a privately owned enterprise, like a rail carrier, which operates in a decentralized manner without coordinating its activities with those of its competitors.

Consequently, as we mentioned earlier, the relevant marginal costs and demand elasticities are those facing the rail carrier whose prices are at issue. And the demand elasticities are those that are produced by market forces, including intermodal, intramodal, source, port and inter-commodity competition.

In markets where these competitive forces are strong, the price that a rail carrier can obtain for its service will be determined by the market. By this we mean, first, that there is a price (sometimes called the 'choke price') above which the rail carrier would find virtually no demand for its service, because shippers would find it less costly to utilize other transportation services, or because receivers would find similar or substitute commodities available at lower delivered prices. Then the railroad has little control over a price if the corresponding choke price is so close to the rail carrier's marginal cost that prices cannot be reduced significantly, without violating the Ramsey condition.

In these circumstances, the Ramsey price is that determined by the market, that is, it is the highest price which enables the rail carrier to obtain any demand for its service, and is greater than or equal to marginal cost. This price is Ramsey efficient in that it induces the traffic to utilize the least costly mode and, at the same time, it provides some non-negative contribution to fixed and common costs. No lower price is more efficient, by the definition we have just given, because the lower price would not stimulate enough increase in traffic to warrant the decrease in mark-up. And a higher price could not be more efficient because it would induce the loss of the traffic to an alternative with greater costs to society, as well as the loss of net revenues that enable the prices of other services to be lower than they would otherwise have to be to yield adequate revenues.

Thus, where competitive forces are sufficiently strong to give control of the prices of rail services to the market, it is those market determined prices that are Ramsey optimal. This finding is consistent with the provision of the Staggers Rail Act that stipulates that prices below a certain percentage of variable costs (160 per cent in 1981) lie outside the direct purview of regulatory oversight. We would interpret this provision to mean that such prices are, in essence, to be determined by the market.

The net revenues derived from such market-determined prices should be subtracted from fixed and common costs to determine adequacy of the net revenues to be obtained from the other services of the rail carrier. The inverse elasticity rule should be then applied to these other services whose prices are not determined by market forces.

The Incentives for Rail Carriers with Adequate Revenues to Levy Ramsey Prices

A rail carrier with adequate revenues earns, in the long run, enough to cover the carrier's cost of capital. There is one principal source of incentives for such a carrier to adopt efficient pricing, even though its net revenues are constrained by regulation just to cover its capital costs and no more.

Such a rail carrier is motivated, perhaps more than other firms in similar circumstances, to maintain its traffic base and to guard against substantial diversion of its traffic to suppliers already in operation or to potential competitors. This is because a large portion of a rail carrier's capital stock is non-fungible, or 'sunk', so that significant losses of traffic would cause losses of revenue far greater than the costs that would thereby be saved. Consequently, a rail carrier with adequate revenues has a particularly compelling incentive to set rates in a manner that will discourage defections of shippers and market erosion to competing suppliers of transportation services, both in the short and in the long run. It may be clear intuitively that among the pricing policies that generate adequate revenues, it is Ramsey pricing that most effectively discourages such defections and market erosion. This is simply because at any one time the Ramsey prices yield shippers the greatest total net benefits possible from prices which yield adequate revenues, and therefore offer shippers the smallest feasible inducement to divert their traffic. In fact, we have elsewhere demonstrated that an enterprise unprotected by any entry barriers can best protect itself from market incursions by competitors by setting its prices at their Ramsey levels.[16]

RAMSEY PRICING IN PRACTICE

While we have explained the virtues and characteristics of public interest (Ramsey) prices in detail, we have not yet discussed a crucial issue relating to their use in practice. That issue is whether there are any significant impediments to the use of Ramsey pricing in practice. In short, the answer is no. Familiar methods of market and cost investigation, using both formal analysis and judgment, can be employed by a rail carrier to choose rates consistent with the Ramsey pricing principles.

As we discussed earlier in the section concerned with Ramsey pricing for a rail carrier that has not yet achieved adequate revenues, the Ramsey prices are those that maximize net revenues. In principle, no inordinate complexity impedes the task of deciding what price for a given service is most likely to yield the highest possible net revenues. In practice, market uncertainties and imperfect information may make this task more difficult. However, it is most important to recognize that the vast majority of firms in our economy face this very same task every day. They handle it by combining information gleaned from such sources as market studies, internal studies of their own costs, economic projections, business planning, customer interactions and experience. Then, based on best available information on demand and costs, formal analysis and business judgment are exercised to choose the prices that most effectively produce net revenues.

Thus, rail carriers with inadequate revenues should be left essentially unconstrained and even encouraged to follow best current business practices in the pursuit of the highest net revenues. Here, the incentives of such rail carriers surely coincide with the public interest in their financial viability. Consequently, regulatory oversight should be confined to periodic assessments to determine whether adequate revenues have yet been achieved.

Rail carriers able to earn adequate revenues with more than one set of prices have genuine choices in deciding whether to set some rates high and others low or whether instead, to set the former rates lower and make up for this by setting the latter rates higher. As we discussed in the final part of the preceding section, for the long run, such a carrier has every incentive to choose the Ramsey prices. However, because these incentives may be less powerful than those inducing a carrier to pursue adequate revenues, it may be appropriate to require rail carriers with adequate revenues to stand ready to show that their new rates for rail dominant services are consistent with the principles of Ramsey pricing.

The necessary elements of such a demonstration are assessments of the elasticities of demand and marginal costs of the carrier's services, other than those sufficiently competitive for their prices to be determined entirely by the market. Of course the rail carriers have much experience in assessing variable costs, and these can provide the basis for workable approximations to marginal costs if the principles outlined in that part of the preceding section concerned with the definition of marginal cost are followed.

Specific Ramsey prices may be calculated for a particular rail carrier. Several things should be kept in mind when calculating those prices.

First, such specific Ramsey prices should be determined for the given rail carrier.

Second, specific Ramsey prices should be determined from up-to-date figures for demand elasticities that will indicate the effects on demand of new price changes. These cannot be supplied entirely by statistical analyses of past market data, but can only be assessed by market experts, who may utilize such analyses in conjunction with their other sources of information.

Third, the specific Ramsey prices will normally differ among different services and movements. Thus, the Ramsey price, or the Ramsey price expressed as a percentage of variable cost that is calculated for an entire category of freight should not be construed as the appropriate rate for each service and movement encompassed by the category. Nevertheless, the Ramsey price for an entire category can be an informative indicator of the average of the Ramsey prices for the movements encompassed by the category. In fact, it can be demonstrated mathematically that the Ramsey price–cost ratios calculated for entire categories of freight are close approximations to the respective averages of the Ramsey price–cost ratios for the individual movements within the categories, if the movements within each category are relatively homogeneous in their elasticities of demand. However, it is important to emphasize that even if the aggregate price–cost ratio is close to the average one, serious inefficiency can be expected to result from the imposition of the same price–cost ratio upon all movements within a given category.

The implications of this discussion can now be summarized. It is ordinary business practice for a firm to choose prices designed to attain maximal net revenues. Certainly, rail carriers with revenues which are as yet inadequate can reliably be expected to pursue this goal, and should be permitted and encouraged to do so. The fundamental building blocks of this decision process, that is, marginal costs and demand elasticities, are also the central determinants of Ramsey prices for a carrier with adequate revenues. Thus, a rail carrier would not be burdened unduly by the process of arriving at Ramsey prices for its services and movements. Well established statistical techniques and other sources of market information can be utilized by a rail carrier in this decision process.

STAND-ALONE COST AS A RATE CEILING

As we have demonstrated, the rate ceilings derived from fully distributed costs are inimical to the public interest.

However, should it prove appropriate to do so, ceilings on rates that are economically rational can be derived from cost calculations. These ceilings are obtainable from the stand-alone cost test, which requires that the revenues from any service or group of services fall below the total cost (including the cost of capital facilities evaluated at the current cost of capital) which would be incurred by supplying that service or group of services in isolation.[17] Rail carriers supply a large number of different services with complementarities in their production (economies of scope) that arise, in part, from the utilization of common facilities. Consequently, the total cost to a carrier of supplying many services simultaneously is less than the sum of the costs of supplying them each in isolation from one another.[18] The stand-alone cost of a service is defined as the cost of supplying that service in isolation. The stand-alone cost of a group of services is the cost of supplying those services, without the supply of any others.

By requiring each service or group of services supplied by a rail carrier to contribute revenues less than stand-alone costs, the test assures each shipper and each group of shippers a share in the benefits derived from simultaneity of production – from economies of scope. Thus, each shipper is guaranteed some benefit from the revenues collected by the carrier from others. The stand-alone cost test offers assurance to each shipper and group of shippers that it will be better off with the existing rates than it would be if it had to fend for itself, as would be the case in the long run if the rail carrier were denied adequate revenues.

The logic of the stand-alone cost test can be explained in another way. In the short run it imposes the same ceilings on rates for any traffic in which the railroad is dominant that the market itself will impose in the long run, and that the market would impose at all times if it were subject to either active or potential rail competition. This follows because, in the long run, no group of shippers would agree to pay more to a carrier for their transportation services than it would cost them to produce these services for themselves. In the short run, a rail carrier facing either active or potential competition could not obtain revenues from a group of shippers that exceeded their stand-alone costs, because those shippers could then be profitably served by a competitor charging lower rates. Thus, the stand-alone cost test affords shippers the same protection that competition would provide.

Consequently, *the stand-alone cost test is unnecessary and inappropriate where there is competition.* However, for any shippers who are truly captive, in that the rail carrier faces no direct, indirect or potential competition for their freight, the stand-alone cost test does provide an economically rational rate ceiling.

The stand-alone cost test is intimately related to the test for the absence of cross-subsidization. Economic analysis holds that a group of services is cross-subsidized if its rates generate revenues that are less than the incremental costs of supplying the services.[19] The incremental costs are those that could be saved by discontinuing the supply of the services.

Obversely, a group of services is not cross-subsidized, or is compensatory, if its revenues cover its incremental costs. As such, compensatory services provide a contribution to common costs, and thereby make it possible for rates for other services to be lower than they would have to be in isolation from the compensatory ones.

Hence, it follows logically that if a carrier's revenues do not exceed total costs, and if all groups of services are compensatory, then it must be true that no group of services is priced above stand-alone costs.[20] After all, if some services were priced excessively high, the excess revenues would have to go somewhere, either producing excessive overall earnings for the carrier or cross-subsidy for some of its other services. Thus, there is a logical indirect way to carry out the stand-alone cost test: *no rate or group of rates can exceed stand-alone costs if overall earnings are not excessive and if all groups of rates are compensatory*.

The indirect test for a carrier whose total revenues are less than total costs is somewhat less stringent: *The revenues from a group of services lie below stand-alone costs if any deficit between the remaining services' revenues and incremental costs is less than the carrier's overall deficit, that is, the difference between its total revenues and total costs*. This follows because if the group of services in question were to generate revenues that exceed their stand-alone costs, that excess would correspondingly reduce the carrier's overall deficit, below the deficit between the remaining services' revenues and incremental costs. Thus, for a carrier without adequate revenues, the presence of some rates that are not compensatory does not, in itself, prove that other rates are excessively high.

Direct application of the stand-alone cost test to a single service requires that its rate be compared with the unit cost that would have to be incurred in the long run if the railroad were to supply no service other than that being tested. However, this test will not impose the strictest ceiling upon the rate if the service utilizes common facilities that are also employed to supply some other services. Then, a stricter ceiling emerges by comparison of the revenues and stand-alone cost of the *group* of services that utilizes these common facilities. Here, the relevant ceiling on the revenue from a service is its variable cost, plus the costs of the common facilities utilized, less the contribution to those costs from the other services that use them.

While the rationale and definition of the stand-alone cost test are straightforward, its direct implementation in practice requires careful distinctions among services. For example, the stand-alone cost for a single movement that travels a significant distance along a main line is likely to be enormous. In such a case the reasoning just outlined suggests that it is appropriate to compare the revenue from the movement not just with its own stand-alone cost, but with its own variable costs, plus the costs of the main line less the contribution to the main line costs from the other movements that travel along it. The practical problem that arises here is the definition and evaluation of the contribution. This is clear for a movement that utilizes no common facilities other than that main line: its contribution is simply the difference between its revenue and the costs (including capital costs) that are directly attributable to it. However, the contribution to the main line costs by a movement that utilizes other common facilities as well is not so clearly defined. Here, any arbitrary allocation of the total contribution among the common facilities that are utilized by such traffic can render the stand-alone cost test an instrument of economic inefficiency. In such a case, the only economically justifiable procedure is either to segregate out all users who do not use only the facilities in question, or to widen the group of movements under consideration further to include all those that utilize the other common facilities. This process may have to be continued until the group encompasses all movements that are confined to a separable portion of the rail network. In some cases, such a group may turn out to be sufficiently large so as to render the test impractical.

We are led by this analysis to conclude that the stand-alone cost test does, in principle, provide appropriate ceilings on rates for traffic in transportation markets without competition. Direct use of the stand-alone cost test may be feasible for groups of movements or services that are confined to a separable portion of the rail network. Otherwise, the indirect form of the test is appropriate. This requires examination of the overall earnings of the rail carrier to determine whether they are excessive, and whether a deficit (relative to incremental costs) is incurred by any group of the carrier's services that is larger than whatever deficit there is for the carrier overall.

SPECIAL SOCIAL GOALS

As we have demonstrated, Ramsey pricing induces the most efficient use of the nation's transportation services and provides the highest net benefits to consumers that are possible from financially viable carriers. However, certain rail services may be deemed to have significant social consequences beyond the benefits they confer on those who purchase them. For example, it is conceivable that a commuter rail service will have significant beneficial effects on the economic development of a region, that rail transport of hazardous materials by railroad may endanger bystanders, or that rail transport of recyclable materials can help to conserve valuable public resources.

Economists label such effects externalities, because their effects are external to the market transactions directly involved. Analysis shows that where the external effects of the use of service are detrimental, the public interest calls for a price that is higher than it would be otherwise, in order to discourage the activity with the undesirable external consequences. Similarly, beneficial externalities call for prices lower than they would otherwise be.

Traditional economic analysis holds that the appropriate public policy entails taxes on activities which generate substantial detrimental externalities and subsidies to activities with beneficial externalities.[21] Pollution taxes, fines for speeding, subsidized treatment of contagious diseases and public education are all examples of such policies. But economists agree that the decision that an activity merits a tax or a subsidy because it causes significant externalities is appropriately made by a legislature or other representative of the public interest, rather than being left to suppliers of the goods or services at issue. Consequently, such a tax or subsidy, where it is deemed appropriate, should be imposed or financed by governmental bodies rather than by the private firms or individuals engaged in the activities.

Thus, rail carriers and consumers of their services should have little, if any, control over the choice of social goals to be served by railroad pricing, aside from efficient utilization of transportation resources. Further, any governmental body that does decide upon the pursuit of a special social goal through railroad pricing or through the supply or the manner of supply of railroad services should be expected to provide the requisite funding. Failure to supply such funding is especially short-sighted if the imposed pursuit of the special social goal impedes the ability of rail carriers to achieve adequate revenues, and thereby impedes the long-run ability of the railroads to provide any service at all.

CONCLUSION

We have described the philosophy of public interest, Ramsey pricing, which is widely accepted by economists and follows the dictates of common sense. We have explained why prices based on fully distributed costs injure the public interest. We have discussed the implications of the public interest, Ramsey pricing philosophy for railroad rates and derived the specific guidelines that should be followed in the place of fully distributed costs. We have indicated how Ramsey pricing can be carried out by rail carriers in practice. We believe that a nation's transportation needs will be well served if the public interest pricing philosophy and its guidelines are accepted and put into practice. Otherwise, there is serious danger that the rail system will end up underfinanced and inefficiently utilized, to the detriment of the national interest.

NOTES AND REFERENCES

1. As put by A. E. Kahn: 'The only economic function of price is to influence behavior. This is a notion that traditional regulators have great difficulty accepting.' *Public Utilities Fortnightly*, 101, 13–17 (19 January 1978). See any economics textbook for a detailed exposition – for example, W. J. Baumol and A. S. Blinder, *Economics: Principles and Policy* (New York: Harcourt, Brace, Jovanovich, 1979) pp. 590–602.
2. This pricing philosophy is today termed Ramsey pricing in honour of the late Frank P. Ramsey, an English economist, mathematician and philosopher, who first derived its basic principles and studied its implications for taxation in 'A Contribution to the Theory of Taxation', *The Economic Journal*, 37, 47–61 (March 1927).
3. See Baumol and Blinder, op. cit., p. 591.
4. There is wide agreement among economists on the inefficiency of prices that are based on 'fully allocated costs'. For example, see J. M. Clark (1923) *Studies in the Economics of Overhead Costs*, p. 14 (Cambridge, Mass.: Ballinger); E. Zajac (1978) *Fairness or Efficiency: An Introduction to Public Utility Pricing*, pp. 86–88; B. M. Owen and R. Braeutigam (1978) *The Regulation Game*, pp. 171–72 (Cambridge, Mass.: Ballinger):

   At this point we will not critique the practice of fully distributed costs further, other than to say that this type of pricing bears no direct relationship to economically efficient pricing since it attempts to set prices based on costs alone, with no consideration for the demand schedules for the service.

5. The absurdity of pricing on the basis of fully distributed costs has long been recognized by economists. The following amusing discussion by a world famous economist appeared more than half a century ago.

   Let us suppose that a travel agency has ordered special trains for a number of Sundays and has contracted to pay 250 *mark* for each train. Each train was to provide 400 seats, all third class. The first Sunday the agency charged 2 *mark* and 125 excursionists bought tickets. The gross receipts amounted to 250 *mark* or to exactly as much as the outlays. The managers of the agency then said to themselves: 'at this price we can only just cover our own costs, but we must also earn something,' and they raised the fare to 3 *mark*. On the next Sunday only 50 people bought tickets. The result was taking in of 150 *mark* and a net loss of 100 *mark*. The agency then reasoned: 'average costs amount to 5 *mark* per person and we carry each passenger for 3 *mark*; we cannot go on like this. The price was raised to 6 *mark* with the result that on the next Sunday the train carried only 6 passengers. The loss rose to 214 *mark*. Now at last the managers of the agency said to themselves: 'this story of costs must be sheer nonsense, for it only ends in losses.' So they reduced the price straight away to 1 *mark*. The result was brilliant: 400 passengers turned up the next Sunday, a profit of 150 *mark* was earned and, strangest of all, costs had fallen to 0.625 *mark* per head.

SOURCE Gustav Cassel, 'The Principles of Railway Rates for Passengers', *International Economic Papers*, No. 6 (1956) translated from *Archive für Eisenbahnwesen*, (1900).

6. The elasticity of demand of a service is defined as the percentage decrease in the quantity demanded in response to a 1 per cent increase in its price.

7. For a survey of derivations and the history of this rule see W. J. Baumol and D. Bradford, 'Optimal Departures From Marginal Cost Pricing,' *American Economic Review*, 60, 265–83 (June 1970). The history dates from at least 1886 (A. T. Hadley, *Railroad Transportation*), and includes such other works as Ramsey, op. cit.; W. A. Lewis, *Overhead Costs* (1949); M. Boiteux, 'Le 'revenue distributable' et les pentes economiquies', *Econometrics*, 19, 112–33 (April 1951); J. Bonbright, *Principles of Public Utility Rates* (1961); and A. E. Kahn, *The Economics of Regulation* (1970). The efficiency properties of Ramsey prices are also discussed by D. Bös, 'Economic Theory of Public Enterprise', (Springer, Heidelberg) (1981); and by J. Finsinger, 'Zur Anatomie von wohl fahrtsoptimalen Preisen für öffentliche Unternehmen', in *Zeitschrift für die gesamte Staatswissenschaft*, 1, 1980, 136–60.

8. Thus, value of service cannot, generally, be evaluated by measures such as the ratio of a commodity's price to its weight.

9. See 7, above. It should be noted that the Ramsey prices satisfy the simplest form of the inverse elasticity rule only if there are no significant cross-elasticities of demand; that is, only if the price of a service affects the demand for only that service, rather than the demands for other services as well. The modification of the inverse elasticity rule to account for significant cross-elasticities was derived by Boiteux, op. cit.; P. Diamond and J. Mirrlees (1971) 'Optimal Taxation and Public Production,' *American Economic Review*, 61, 8–27 and 261–278; and others. As noted by Baumol and Bradford, '[the modification] complicates the analysis but does not change its nature in any fundamental way.' (op. cit., p. 270).

10. In fact, as noted in Baumol and Bradford, op. cit., p. 278, Ramsey prices were characterized by Hadley during the nineteenth century as 'not charging what the traffic cannot bear'.

11. The reason that such balanced reductions in consumption from the ideal level are more efficient than unbalanced ones is the following: as a price is

raised above marginal cost to provide more of the needed net revenues, the quantity of the service that is demanded will decrease from its ideal level and cause a loss of net social benefits. This loss accelerates as the quantity that is demanded decreases, because each succeeding unit of demand that is curtailed has a higher value to consumers. Each curtailed unit has an increasingly higher value because consumers, in their own interests, curtail consumption with low value to themselves first, and then, as prices continue to rise, curtail consumption of units with higher value. As a consequence, the loss of net social benefits resulting from the first units curtailed is minimal because the value of these units to consumers is close to the marginal cost of providing them. However, the loss is more substantial for units that are curtailed from a quantity level that is further from the ideal level demanded at marginal cost prices. Thus, there is a greater loss of net social benefits from a large change in the quantity of a single service than there is, in total, from small changes in the quantities of several services. For any uneven pattern of changes, there is a balanced pattern that yields the same total net revenues and that yields greater net benefits to consumers.

12. These relationships are precise where demands are linear functions of prices and costs are linear functions of quantities. Otherwise these relationships hold only approximately. See E. Zajac, 'Note on an Extension of the Ramsey Inverse Elasticity of Demand Pricing or Taxation Formula', *Journal of Public Economics*, 3, 191–84 (1974), and Baumol and Bradford, op. cit.

13. See R. D. Willig, 'Pareto-superior Nonlinear Outlay Schedules', *The Bell Journal of Economics*, 9, 56–69 (Spring 1978).

14. See R. Braeutigam, (1979) 'Optimal Pricing With Intermodal Competition', *American Economic Review*, 69, 38–49.

15. W. J. Baumol, J. C. Panzar and R. D. Willig (1982) *Contestable Markets and the Theory of Industry Structure* (New York: Harcourt, Brace, Jovanovich).

16. W. J. Baumol, E. D. Bailey and R. D. Willig, 'Weak Invisible Hand Theorems on the Sustainability of Prices in a Multiproduct Monopoly,' *American Economic Review*, 67, 350–65 (June 1977).

17. This test is generally accepted in the economics literature. For example, see Kahn, op. cit., vol. II, p. 222; G. R. Faulhaber, 'Cross-Subsidization: Pricing in Public Enterprises', *American Economic Review*, 65, 966–77 (1975); and Zajac, op. cit., pp. 88–89.

18. See R. D. Willig, 'Multiproduct Technology and Market Structure', *American Economic Review*, 79, 346–51 (May 1979).

19. See Faulhaber, op. cit. and R. D. Willig (1980) 'What Can Markets Control?', in *Perspectives on Postal Service Issues*, R. Sherman (ed.) (Washington, DC: American Enterprise Institute).

20. See Faulhaber, op. cit.

21. The classic treatment is A. C. Pigou (1928) *A Study of Public Finance*, (3rd edn) (London: Macmillan, 1947).

3 On the Contestability of Airline Markets: Some Further Evidence

ELIZABETH E. BAILEY, DANIEL P. KAPLAN and DAVID S. SIBLEY

INTRODUCTION

A key element in determining the degree of inherent contestability of markets is the presence and extent of entry barriers. In US aviation markets, the entry barriers historically imposed by the Civil Aeronautics Board have been largely removed. However, it is thought that other entry barriers – barriers caused by historically determined feed advantages and airport access restrictions – may still prevent airline markets from being contestable. This chapter examines some recent evidence on the extent to which such barriers are currently significant in US aviation markets. The work represents a second effort at examining the degree of contestability of aviation markets during the transition to deregulation.[1]

CONTESTABILITY THEORY

The concept of contestable markets as presented by Baumol, Panzar and Willig,[2] offers a generalization of the theory of pure competition. Under both concepts, potential entrants are assumed to face the same set of productive techniques and market demands as those available to incumbent firms. A key assumption of both theories is that there is frictionless free entry and exit with no special costs that must be borne by

48

an entrant that do not fall on incumbents as well. The purely competitive model assumes that there is such a large number of firms in the market that each considers its production decision has no effect on market prices. By contrast, in a contestable market both incumbents and potential entrants recognize that there may be economies of scale or scope in their markets that limit the number of firms actually serving in the market.

In a contestable market, therefore, firms know that they may have power over prices. A firm will enter the market if it is possible to obtain a positive profit by undercutting the incumbent's price and serving the entire market demand at a new lower price. If the incumbent readjusts price, reducing it beneath that of the entrant, then the new competitor can readily exit from the market without loss of investment, provided that there were no sunk costs of entry.

Although contestable markets may contain only a few firms, they exhibit efficiency properties similar to those in purely competitive models. Firms producing any given product select output levels at which marginal costs of all firms are equal. Moreover, these marginal costs must equal the market price of that product, so that economic profits are zero when there are constant returns to scale locally. Thus, regulatory intervention is not needed in contestable markets even if such markets have some monopoly characteristics.

REGULATORY HISTORY

Aviation regulation in the domestic US had served to undermine contestability properties that the markets might have exhibited in the absence of regulation. The Civil Aeronautics Board (CAB) restricted both entry into the industry and entry by those in the industry into each others city-pair markets.

The structure of the US aviation industry was, in large measure, shaped by a congressionally directed grandfathering of route rights to carriers who enjoyed such rights under air mail contracts. This is shown in Table 3.1 where carriers present in 1938 were still dominant in 1977. Over the next four decades, the aviation industry grew tremendously, with mail accounting eventually for only a small percentage of revenues. Yet governmentally mandated entry barriers continued. The Board's route case programme generally followed general economic conditions with a lag. In periods of high traffic growth and carrier profits, the Board tended to authorize new service of the first non-stop or first competitive

TABLE 3.1   *Revenue passenger-miles in scheduled domestic service, 1938 and 1977*

Carrier	Revenue passenger-miles (billions)	Percent of total
1938		
American Airlines	0.141	29.6
United Airlines	0.109	22.9
Trans World Airlines	0.072	15.1
Eastern Airlines	0.071	14.9
All others	0.083	17.5
Total	0.476	100.0
1977		
United	25.00	20
American	17.12	14
Delta	14.64	12
Trans World	13.16	11
Eastern	12.70	10
Northwest	6.00	5
Western	5.86	5
Continental	5.53	4
Braniff	4.88	4
National	4.22	3
Pan American	1.53	1
All local service	13.54	11
Total	123.09	100

SOURCE   *Air Carrier Traffic Statistics*, May 1977; *Annual Airline Statistics*, Domestic Carriers, 1938.

variety, after lengthy hearing processes. Almost no new authorizations were granted for routes that already had two or more authorized carriers. In periods of poor traffic growth and profitability, the Board tended to authorize very little new service and, particularly, it would not approve new service that would have a competitive impact on incumbent carriers.

Throughout the decades, the Board authorized no new trunk carriers. A system of regional carriers specializing in feeder service, each of which was given a regional monopoly, was established in the 1940s and 1950s. Over time, these subsidized carriers were permitted to compete to a limited extent with trunks in medium density, medium stage length, city-pair markets.

Thus the situation in 1977–78 was an implicit contract that gave local service carriers monopoly rights in their regions, with long-haul traffic turned over as feed to the trunk carriers. Large trunk carriers were, in turn, protected from added competition over the major trunk routes they operated, but could not themselves get any new routes readily.

Because the CAB's policy constituted an almost insuperable barrier to entry, price regulation was required. In the early years of CAB regulation carriers tended to set fares at or near the rail-Pullman level (see Figure 3.1). Rates were generally based on a market's distance, and a mileage taper was introduced in 1952, allowing average fare per passenger mile to decline with distance and thus be somewhat related to costs. Just as with route awards, the CAB tended to be more liberal in approving discount fares when the industry was growing and profitable. As Figure 3.1 shows, prices tended to fall in real terms as technological advances in the airframe industry (such as the introduction of jets in the

* Deflated by implicit deflator — GNP, adjusted to 1938 base
† 1974 data for first nine months

NOTE   The revenue from air operations and revenue shares of the eleven major US airlines are shown in Table 3.1. Five of the carriers controlled 68 per cent of the group's total revenue, but no single company dominated the group.

FIGURE   3.1   *Average fare per passenger mile*

SOURCE   US Congress, Report of the Subcommittee on Administrative Practice and Procedure (1975).

1960s) reduced the cost of providing service. Rate of return regulation for the industry was introduced by the CAB in the 1960s. It was not until the 1970s that the CAB adopted as well a load factor standard (55 per cent and standard seating configurations) to be used in the determination of fare levels, and a comprehensive prescription of the normal fare structure, together with rules governing discount fares.

Although the CAB felt it was administering careful regulation, the structural competitiveness of the industry and the anomalies of regulation both became clear. In the area of pricing, there arose intrastate carriers, free of the federal pricing mandates, who offered high-frequency, low-fare services at approximately half the price level of the certificated carriers. In the interstate markets, where the CAB could control price but not capacity, carriers competed away through service competition the profits that would otherwise have accrued from a pricing policy that was intended to permit long-haul routes to subsidize short-haul routes. In short-haul markets, fares that would have led to losses at a 55 per cent load factor, were either avoided by exit from the markets or were converted into profitable fares by carriers cutting back capacity and raising load factors. As an *ad hoc* remedy to its general policy of constraining short-haul fares below cost, the CAB granted to local service carriers a 30 per cent zone of upward fare flexibility. As evidence mounted that regulation was having perverse consequences, academics began advocating that the regulatory decision structure should be dismantled.[3]

Political and economic forces come together in the mid-1970s. Both pointed toward reduced rather than enhanced regulation for the industry. The Kennedy oversight hearings of 1975 emphasized the principle of getting government out of economic intervention in an industry that appeared to have the potential to be structurally competitive. The hearings promoted the view that the cost of air service could be significantly reduced through deregulation. The hearings also dramatized the lack of openness and of impartiality in the Board's route and enforcement policies; the lack was most notable during the route moratorium of the early 1970s.[4] The Board formed a special advisory task force, which also propounded the merits of regulatory reform.[5]

By October 1978, an Airline Deregulation Act was passed with the joint sponsorship of Senators Cannon and Kennedy. It was supported by the CAB and at least some portions of the industry. The legislation ensured that after a short transition period, there would be complete freedom of route entry and eventually, complete freedom of pricing. It was anticipated that there might be a speed-up in the move of jet service out of small communities, so a system was set up to ensure an 'essential' level of air service for such towns for a ten-year period. The commuter industry was expected to provide this service, without subsidy in most cases, but with subsidy for communities enplaning less than thirty passengers per day.

REMOVAL OF CAB IMPOSED ENTRY BARRIERS

Within six months of the passage of the Deregulation Act, the CAB had moved to substantially open entry. Under new procedures, there were delays of from only one to three months in the granting of new route authority explicitly requested. Moreover, all carriers that applied for a given route were granted authority, though it was recognized that not all carriers granted authority would actually serve. Rather, the CAB's policy provided enough route authority for potential competitors to enter virtually any domestic route. Within a year after the passage of the deregulation act, entry barriers for trunk and local service carriers in aviation markets could no longer be attributed to restrictive licensing policies of the CAB.

Entry barriers at the industry level were also removed. Indeed, the fastest growing segment of the industry under deregulation has been the 'low-cost', newly-certificated jet airlines. Some of these carriers, such as Pacific Southwest Airlines, Air Florida and Southwest Airlines, previously served only intrastate markets, and began moving into interstate markets after deregulation. Other carriers, such as Capitol and World Airways, moved from charter into both scheduled and charter service. Other jet carriers began operations afresh, such as Midway Airlines, New York Air and Peoples Express.[6] Like the local service carriers, these new entrants tend to use small jet aircraft and specialize in relatively short-haul markets. These carriers offer no-frills, high-frequency, low-cost service. New entry has also abounded in the commuter industry.

Full pricing freedom has come more slowly. For the first year prior to deregulation, the Board under the leadership of Alfred Kahn, began to adopt a liberal zone of downward pricing flexibility under which virtually all discount fares were automatically granted. However, throughout 1978 and 1979, the pricing formulas were still in effect as ceilings for both trunk and local service carriers. The disparity between the ceiling levels for the two types of carriers is what permitted Bailey and Panzar to test the effect that potential competition by trunk carriers was having on the pricing behaviour of the local service carriers. In May 1980, the Board made a dramatic move to add upward pricing flexibility lifting the ceiling in markets less than 200 miles, and granting 50 per cent and 30 per cent upward fare flexibility in 201–400 mile and 401 + mile markets, respectively. On 14 September 1980, this was amended to grant $15 plus 30 per cent upward pricing flexibility in all markets. As a result, we are now in a position to examine the contestability hypothesis somewhat more thoroughly than was possible before.

OTHER POTENTIAL ENTRY BARRIERS

We look here at two types of evidence about possible entry barriers in aviation markets other than of the purely route authority variety. Both examine measures of concentration in the industry itself and at the level of city-pair route markets since deregulation. We will draw upon two studies which the CAB will shortly submit to Congress.[7] Figure 3.2 provides evidence that new entry is not only potentially possible but is serving in actual practice to reduce the degree of concentration in the industry. The diagram shows that there has been a substantial increase in the shift of market shares since 1977. Truck carrier share is declining markedly while there have been net gains for the local service carriers, the new intrastate jet carriers and the commuters.

At the city-pair level, a more varied picture emerges. Table 3.2 shows changes in market concentration of nonstop flights by market density and distance for the top 100 origin and destination (O and D) markets, the next 100 largest markets and a random sample of smaller markets. (The top 200 markets account for roughly 95 per cent of total domestic revenue passenger miles.) The time periods displayed are November 1978 (the time of passage of the Airline Deregulation Act) and November 1980. The index of concentration used is a Herfindahl index for departures. For the top 100 markets, concentration fell at all distances except for markets of less than 200 miles, so that average concentration in 1980 was only 93.3 per cent of what it was in 1978. In the second 100 markets, concentration fell in all markets. For small markets, average concentration was slightly less in 1980 than 1978 despite the exit by certificated carriers from these routes. This is due to expansion of commuter airlines. Table 3.3 is complementary to Table 3.2, and shows net entry and exit for these markets. For markets in the top 100, net entry was positive in the overwhelming majority of cases. This holds true for the second 100 markets, too, except for markets with distance between 0 and 200 miles. In this last category, markets with net

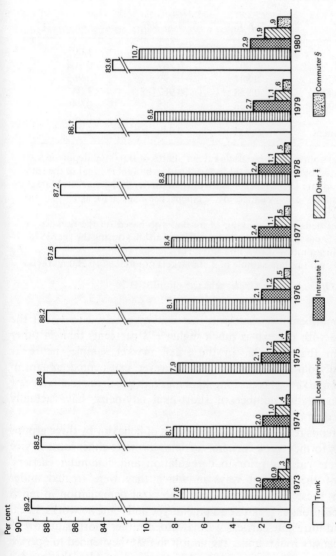

Per cent

* Represents revenue passenger miles for domestic scheduled certificated and commuter carriers.
† Represents newly certificated former intrastate carriers.
‡ Includes all domestic scheduled certificated carriers other than trunks, locals, and certificated former intrastate and commuter carriers.
§ Includes newly certificated former commuters.

FIGURE 3.2 *Changes in market share of traffic,* * *calendar years 1973–80*

TABLE 3.2   *Changes in market concentration* of non-stop flights by market density and distance November 1978 to November 1980*

(*Average of ratios of 1980 Herfindahl to 1978 Herfindahl*)

Distance	Top 100	Density† Second 100	Small markets‡
0–200	1.192	0.987	1.003
201–500	0.907	0.869	0.964
501–1000	0.897	0.999	0.965
1001–1500	0.958	0.967	1.046
1501–2000	0.938	0.985	0.946
2000 +	0.962	0.982	0.969
All distances	0.933	0.949	0.981

* Market concentration reflects carrier shares of non-stop departures as measured by the Herfindahl Index. The Herfindahl is equal to the sum of the square of the market share of each carrier in the market. Market Herfindahls are weighted by segment passengers to arrive at cell averages.

† Market density is a ranking of market size based on the number of O and D passengers carried by certificated airlines during the year 1978. It excludes intra-Alaska and intra-Hawaii markets.

‡ Based on a random sample of 230 markets not in the top 200 markets.

SOURCE *Official Airline Guide*, selected months, 1978–80.

entry outnumbered markets with net exit by nearly 2 to 1, but the percentage with net exit is much higher (38 per cent) than in other markets in the top 300. In the small market sample, net exits substantially outnumber net entries. However, exit is predominant in short-haul markets whereas long-haul markets, which are relatively few in relation to the number of short-haul city-pairs, have actually experienced entry.

These trends reflect rather distinct types of behavior by three groups of carriers: former trunk carriers, carriers who were either local service or intrastate carriers prior to deregulation and commuter carriers. Because of the different ways in which they were treated under regulation, these two groups began the era of deregulation in much different positions as regards equipment type and route networks. Local service and intrastate carriers were awarded rather short-haul, low to medium density routes under regulation so that they tended to operate two-engine jet equipment with 100–120 seats or less. Also, they tended to have dense short-haul route systems near large hub airports, where they had handed off long distance traffic to the trunk carriers. Since

TABLE 3.3 *Changes in number of carriers offering non-stop jet service by market density and distance* (*Markets with net entry and net exit by large jet aircraft operators,* * *November 1978 to November 1980*)

| | Top 100 | | | Second 100 | | | Small markets‡ | | |
Distance	Entry	Exit	No change	Entry	Exit	No change	Entry	Exit	No change
0–200	2 / 40%	0	3 / 60%	5 / 62%	3 / 38%	0	9 / 10%	30 / 32%	54 / 58%
201–500	12 / 39%	6 / 19%	13 / 42%	10 / 31%	3 / 9%	19 / 59%	7 / 10%	27 / 39%	36 / 51%
501–1000	14 / 54%	0.	12 / 46%	10 / 32%	3 / 10%	18 / 58%	4 / 14%	7 / 24%	18 / 62%
1001–1500	8 / 47%	1 / 6%	8 / 47%	2 / 17%	1 / 8%	9 / 75%	3 / 25%	0	9 / 75%
1500 +	6 / 35%	1 / 6%	10 / 59%	1 / 7%	0	14 / 93%	2 / 33%	0	4 / 66%
All markets	42 / 44%	8 / 8%	46 / 48%	28 / 29%	10 / 10%	60 / 61%	25 / 12%	64 / 31%	121 / 58%

* A market is defined to have had net entry when there are more carriers present in the market in November 1980 than November 1979. Similarly a market had net exit when there are less carriers present.

† Market density is a ranking of market size based on the number of O and D passengers carried by certificated airlines during the year 1978. It excludes intra-Alaska and intra-Hawaii markets.

‡ Based on a random sample of 230 markets not in the top 200 markets.

SOURCE *Official Airline Guide,* selected months, 1978–80.

deregulation and with the simultaneous rise in fuel prices, local service carriers' equipment has turned out to be quite efficient and they have dropped some very thin routes and have configured their local short-haul systems so as to support greatly expanded long-haul operations. In general, local service carriers have moved substantially into markets above 500 miles in distance. The former trunk carriers began deregulation with large equipment and strong positions at major hub airports (an exception is Delta, which had efficient B-727-200 equipment to serve its short-haul system around Atlanta as well as larger equipment for long distance markets). As a group, the trunks have shifted capacity into markets over 1000 miles and have dropped many routes to small hub or non-hub airports. As trunks and local carriers have moved out of the very thinnest markets, commuters have moved in, using the rather small turbo-prop equipment which is most efficient for these markets.

The discussion, so far, has been purely descriptive. However, these aggregate data do tell us something about whether or not it is plausible to believe that entry barriers are high at the city-pair level. If important entry barriers exist, then high concentration in a market should persist for a substantial period of time, since the function of an entry barrier must be to preserve dominant firms' positions in concentrated markets. Hence, one test of the height of entry barriers is to see if highly concentrated markets *stay* highly concentrated, or whether they become relatively unconcentrated within a short period of time (the reverse is true for initially unconcentrated markets). Working from the top 200 markets, the Herfindahl in a market of average density and distance which was monopolized in the fourth quarter of 1979 (that is, a Herfindahl Index for departures of 1.0) falls, on average to 0.59 one year later. With a slightly lower Herfindahl Index of 0.8, in 1979 the Herfindahl fell to 0.565 by the end of 1980. With a Herfindahl of 0.60, the index fell 10.5 points within one year. Although not conclusive by itself, this finding suggests clearly that entry barriers are not so high that a carrier with a large market share in a given city-pair market can regard itself as being immune from significant entry by new carriers or expansion of service by other incumbent carriers.

This finding makes the premise behind the innate contestability of airline markets quite believable. If highly concentrated city-pair markets are subject to such rapid deconcentration, then it is entirely reasonable to suppose that a carrier serving a given market views potential entry (including expansion of output by incumbents) as a force tempering his ability to raise fares above cost. It seems much less plausible to suppose that entry barriers are high enough so that measures of market concentration – at least for city-pair markets – constitute a reliable indicator of market power by incumbent carriers.

A third area of concern is whether or not there are market barriers at certain large hub airports. Some of these airports have highly concentrated feed networks controlled by one or a few carriers. Some are also subject to access restrictions.

Out of all the large hub airports in the US, there are seven which are especially worrisome. These seven connecting hubs along with the percentage of feed traffic kept online by carriers at each hub are displayed in Table 3.4. The proportion of feed traffic kept on line is often used as an indicator of the extent to which the dominant carriers at a hub are able to control both feeder and long-haul routes out of a given connecting hub. Of these airports, it should be noted that O'Hare is an access-constrained airport, exemplified by the presence of slot constraints there. For this reason, we should expect fares in markets out of Chicago to be higher than in similar markets which do not involve access-constrained airports. This would come about simply because the slot system imposes an artificial limit on supply, and not necessarily because carriers at Chicago possess the market power to set prices above

TABLE 3.4

Airport	Concentration of emplanements*	Percent feed kept online†
Atlanta	0.66	0.77
Pittsburgh	0.64	0.68
Dallas–Ft. Worth	0.51	0.40
Denver	0.50	0.65
Minneapolis–St. Paul	0.45	0.55
Chicago–O'Hare	0.43	0.48
St. Louis	0.52	0.64

Major carriers at hubs.
Denver: Frontier, Delta, Continental, United
Atlanta: Delta, Eastern
St. Louis: Ozark, TWA, American
Minneapolis–St. Paul: Northwest, Republic
Chicago–O'Hare: United, American
Dallas–Ft. Worth: Texas International, Braniff, Delta
Pittsburgh: USAir
* 1980, fourth quarter.
† 1980, third quarter.

cost. It has also been argued that Atlanta had very tight groundside access during our sample period and was congested on the airside as well. Therefore, if Atlanta fares were higher than other fares, this could, again, be due simply to higher costs for access and not to price-setting power on the parts of Delta and Eastern, the major carriers at Atlanta. On the other hand, higher fares *could* represent market power conferred by the tight control of feed traffic around Atlanta by Delta and Eastern. It could also be that market power exists out of Atlanta *because* of groundside constraints which could make it difficult for carriers other than Delta and Eastern to put more than a negligible number of feed routes into Atlanta to support competitive long-haul service.[8]

With this in mind, in the third and fourth quarters of 1980, both Atlanta and O'Hare had fares which were higher than the average in a sample of 181 large markets, according to usual standards of statistical significance.[9] None of the other airports had fares which were significantly different from the sample average. What can be concluded from this?

First, the O'Hare result is more likely due to scarce access than to market power. In fact, O'Hare is the least concentrated of the seven major connecting hubs and carriers at O'Hare retained a lower proportion of their traffic online than did the carriers at any of the others. On the others hand, the presence of slot constraints indicates that fares out of Chicago should be relatively high even without any market power.

The fact that Atlanta fares are significantly higher than average is consistent with arguments linking market power to control at a major connecting hub, although it does not dispose of the issue. Certainly, Atlanta is prolific compared to all other hubs (except Pittsburgh), in its level of concentration and its online feed percentage, which are both far above the levels achieved at other major connecting hubs.

The example of Pittsburgh, however, shows that one cannot uncritically link high hub concentration with market power. Concentration of enplanements at Pittsburgh is extremely high – very close to concentration at Atlanta and far above concentration at any of the others. Its percentage of feed kept online is second only to Atlanta's (although not much higher than that of St. Louis or Dallas–Fort Worth). Furthermore, USAir has used its system of Allegheny Commuters to build its Pittsburgh operation into a classic hub-and-spoke system. Nonetheless, although Pittsburgh fares were higher than average, the difference was not statistically significant, or even close to it, in either the third or the fourth quarter of 1980. Thus, it appears that even in the early years after deregulation, the concentration at major hub airports may not lead to the ability to exercise market power.

TRENDS IN FARE STRUCTURE

It is also possible to examine the transition to contestability by looking at fares directly. Looking at average coach fare as a percentage of the DPFI fare, the CAB has found that this percentage declines with distance, both for large and small markets. In thin markets of less than 500 miles, average coach fares rose substantially above the DPFI but dipped below the DPFI for longer distances. Comparing small markets with large markets, fares are uniformly higher in the small markets. This reflects the fact that carriers in thin markets can only maintain schedule quality by using small aircraft, which have a relatively high cost per available seat mile. Averaging over all distances, the thicker the market, the lower its fare as a percentage of the DPFI. Table 3.5 illustrates these points.

The efficiency of the current fare structure is particularly noticeable in tourist markets. In tourist markets, most passengers are travelling on fares with advance purchase and other restrictions which combine to make traffic more predictable for airlines. Also, tourists are less sensitive to schedule frequency than are other travellers. For these reasons, carriers in tourist markets can operate larger aircraft at higher load factors than in other markets. Therefore, average fares in tourist markets are lower (as a percentage of DPFI) than are fares in other markets as we see in Table 3.6. Tables 3.5 and 3.6 show that fares are responding to costs and market conditions somewhat more than they

TABLE 3.5   *Average fare as a percent of DPFI formula in 1980*

	Market size		
Market distance	Top 100 markets	Second 100 markets	Smaller markets
0–200	92	94	123
201–500	94	93	112
501–1000	92	91	99
1001–1500	80	87	93
1500 +	74	81	91
Average of all Distances	87	90	112

TABLE 3.6   *Fares, load factors and aircraft size: long-haul tourist markets v. all long-haul markets, 1980*

	Market size		
	Top 100 markets	*Second 100 markets*	*Smaller markets*
Fares as per cent DPFI:			
all markets	74	81	89
tourist markets	65	70	80
Average load factor:			
all markets	59	54	57
tourist markets	67	61	61
Average aircraft size:			
all markets	237	207	181
tourist markets	274	292	200

did under the DPFI. There clearly remains, however, the ability to price discriminate between business and leisure travel.

There also remains the fact that actual (rather than potential) competition is often serving to discipline prices. This can be seen in the periodic fare wars that have taken place in the major US coast-to-coast markets. There is also analytic evidence that there remains a relationship between concentration and prices. Estimating equations in which price is taken to be a function of distance, density, airport access constraints, the tourist nature of the market and the Herfindahl index, find that the coefficient of the concentration variable is positive and significant.[10] Thus, a positive relationship probably continues to exist between concentration at the city-pair level and the average fare. Thus, a fully contestable marketplace has not yet been achieved in US aviation markets.

SUMMARY

This paper has reviewed some recently developed evidence on entry barriers and fares in the post-deregulation period. The entry data suggest strongly that entry barriers are low at the hub and city-pair level. The evidence on fares may be interpreted to show that carriers in highly concentrated markets still have a modest amount of price-setting power.

One can make an analogy between the structure of the Western European aviation system, as a whole, and the US domestic system prior to deregulation. Since each flag carrier has a monopoly within its own country, it has some of the features of a local service carrier under CAB regulation, which had a monopoly within a certain region of the United States. The routes *between* European countries and to the rest of the world mean that the European carriers have some of the features of the US trunk carriers. If one could imagine a deregulated European airline industry, then there is reason to expect that it might evolve in a similar pattern to the US, and with similar overall results. It would not be unreasonable to expect that each country's carrier would maintain and improve its network design, retaining a high proportion of feed traffic online, that there would be a proliferation of discount fares, and that there might be established some new low-fare, point-to-point services (and carriers) who would compete with the services provided by the traditional flag carriers.

NOTES AND REFERENCES

The views expressed in this chapter are those of the authors, and not necessarily those of the Civil Aeronautics Board.

1. The earlier work showed that despite the presence of economies of density in city-pair airline markets, potential competition is effectively policing the pricing behavior of the local service carriers in their medium and long-haul routes. See Elizabeth E. Bailey and John C. Panzar, 'The Contestability of Airline Markets During the Transition to Deregulation', *Law and Contemporary Problems*, 44, 125–45 (Winter 1981).
2. William J. Baumol, John C. Panzar and Robert D. Willig, *Contestable Markets and the Theory of Industry Structure*, (1981).
3. See, for example, George Douglas and James Miller (1974) *Economic Regulation of Domestic Air Transport* (Washington: Brookings Institution) and William A. Jordan (1972) *Airline Regulation in America: Effects and Imperfections*, (Baltimore: Johns Hopkins Press, 1972).
4. See 'Oversight of Civil Aeronautics Board Practices and Procedures', US Congress, Senate Committee on the Judiciary, Hearings before the Subcommittee on Administrative Practice and Procedures, 1975.
5. R. Pulsifer, L. S. Keyes, P. Eldridge, J. A. McMahon and W. L. Demory (1975) *Report of the CAB Special Staff on Regulatory Reform* (US Civil Aeronautics Board, July).
6. At present, several more carriers on the model of Southwest and Midway are either applying for certification or are close to inaugurating service: Air Chicago, Air International, Columbia Air, Muse Air and Sun Pacific.

64 *Deregulation*

7. David Sibley *et al.* (1981) *Antitrust Policy for the Deregulated Airline Industry* (Washington, DC: Civil Aeronautics Board, July) and David R. Graham and Daniel P. Kaplan (1981) *CAB Report on Developments in the Deregulated Airline Industry* (Washington, DC: Civil Aeronautics Board, July).
8. See Sibley, op. cit.
9. See Sibley, op. cit.
10. In addition, to the previously cited studies, see also Sibley, D., D. Graham and D. Kaplan (1981) 'The Emerging Competitive Structure of the Deregulated Airline Industry', presented at the European Association for Research in Industrial Economics, Basle, Switzerland, September 10–18. They find that this relationship between concentration and fares is only shortrun in nature.

Part III
Insurance Markets

4 Misinformation and Equilibrium in Insurance Markets

PAUL R. KLEINDORFER and HOWARD KUNREUTHER[1]

INTRODUCTION

This chapter is concerned with the role of misinformation by firms and consumers with respect to the selling and buying of insurance. Our interest is in the relationship between the accuracy of consumer beliefs and the relative performance of the market system and social program- mes. Such an investigation requires us to determine under what conditions a stable market equilibrium exists and, if it does, what type of insurance policies are offered to consumers. We can then contrast these market outcomes with premium regulation or some form of required insurance coverage.

There are two reasons we are focusing on consumer misinformation in this paper. First, there is considerable evidence from recent laboratory experiments and field survey data that individuals systematically mis- estimate probabilities particularly when they are relatively low, the type of situation where insurance is most relevant (see Kunreuther *et al.*, 1978; Fischhoff, Slovic and Lichtenstein, 1978). Secondly, economists have focused almost entirely on firm misinformation and implicitly assumed that consumer misperception only affects individuals adversely but has little impact on market behavior.

The results of our analysis suggest that this may not be the case. We show that the existence and efficiency of competitive insurance markets can be affected by consumer (mis)perceptions of the risks that are being insured against. For example, we show that underestimation of the probability of insurable events by high-risk individuals may adversely affect the existence of competitive equilibrium.

The paper is in the spirit of recent work in economics which deals with accuracy and asymmetries in information between the consumer and the firm where insurance is used as a prototype example (see Arrow, 1963; Williamson, 1975). If the consumer knows more about his risk than the supplier, then problems of adverse selection may result where only the highest risk group is offered coverage unless special steps are taken by the insurer. Such adverse selection problems brought on by insurers' lack of information on customer characteristics will be one feature of the model developed below. Our specific interest is to determine what additional problems consumer misperceptions may cause in such a world.

As an example, the reader may wish to think of automobile insurance under conditions where firms do not know the accident probabilities for each of their customers. Alternatively, firms may be prevented by law from using information (for example, geographic location) which would properly classify customers according to their respective risk class. Customers, in turn, may misperceive their probabilities of being involved in an accident. Under these conditions, and assuming free entry and exit (no fixed costs) of insurance firms into this market, we are interested in determining what sort of policies, if any, would be marketed in the absence of regulation.

Rothschild and Stiglitz (1976) suggest an ingenious way to overcome the adverse selection problem. Rather than specifying a premium rate per dollar, firms would offer a set of policies $\{ < p_j, Q_j > \, | \, j = 1, 2, \ldots, J \,\}$, consisting of a premium per dollar (p_j) and a stated amount of coverage (Q_j).[2] In this way the rate could differ between high and low coverage. Given this system of insurance they investigate under what situations a stable (Nash) competitive equilibrium exists. One of the most important results of their analysis is that there cannot be a pooled equilibrium (that is, a single market-wide policy) which is stable. In the case of two risk groups, an equilibrium, if it exists, consists of two separate policies with different premiums and different stated coverage. Wilson (1977) independently investigated the same problem as Rothschild and Stiglitz (hereafter referred to as R–S), but utilized a different definition of equilibrium which involved some foresight on the part of firms.

The contrast between the two types of equilibrium is instructive. In a traditional Nash equilibrium, each firm (including potential entrants) is assumed to determine the set of policies it will offer under the assumption that all other firms make no changes in their current offerings. Each policy is on the actuarially fair odds line so that no firm can enter the market and make a profit by offering a policy to either high- or low-risk group. In the Wilson equilibrium each firm determines its optimal set of policy offerings under the assumption that any currently marketed policies which become unprofitable as a result of new offerings will no longer be offered in the market place. Thus, an equilibrium in Wilson's sense requires that firms look ahead far enough to evaluate the consequences of new policy offerings on the profitability of all currently marketed policies. Clearly, it would be empirically and theoretically of interest to determine when the Wilson assumptions on firm behavior are justified. In this paper, however, we shall simply analyze the implications of the Nash and Wilson assumptions when consumer misperceptions are present. This is intended as a prelude to an empirical study of other aspects of firm and consumer decision processes in insurance markets (see, for example, Kleindorfer and Kunreuther, 1981, and Finsinger, 1983, in this regard).

Miyasaki (1977) has studied the Wilson equilibrium in detail. When there are two risk classes, a high- and a low-risk group, the Miyasaki results imply that the Wilson equilibrium will not be a pooled equilibrium, as R–S and Wilson had both originally, but erroneously, thought. Rather it will consist of a pair of contracts, one directed toward the high-risk and the other directed toward the low-risk individuals. This is just the same as for the Nash equilibrium, which (for this case with two risk groups) also consists of a pair of policies whenever it exists. Indeed, whenever the separating Nash equilibrium exists, it coincides with the Wilson equilibrium and all consumers pay actuarially fair premia. When the Nash separating equilibrium fails to exist, however, the Wilson equilibrium will still exist, but it will now entail a pair of insurance policies being marketed such that low-risk individuals will subsidize high-risk persons.

Miyasaki's work is related to labour market theory where firms could not distinguish between high productivity (that is, low risk) and low productivity (that is, high risk) workers. Spence (1978) translated Miyasaki's model to the insurance market context and generalized the model to accommodate *n* different groups. His analysis provides a parsimonious mathematical framework for analyzing the existence of Nash–Wilson equilibria and the associated cross-subsidization issues involved. More recently Dahlby (1981) provided a graphical procedure for determining Nash–Wilson equilibria and for analyzing the degree of subsidy which the low risk group provides to the high-risk group in equilibrium. Our discussion of the characteristics of an equilibrium will build on these three papers, (henceforth referred to as M–S–D). None of these studies investigated the implications of consumer misperceptions on market stability and welfare.

There is an underlying rationale in the back of equilibrium analysis which enables us to generalize the above studies to the case where there are n different risk groups and within each group there may be multiple subgroups having different misperceptions of the probability of a loss. This rationale consists of two very simple principles. Firstly, existing firms must offer policies yielding zero expected profits and which maximize the perceived expected utility of the lowest risk group over all feasible (that is, zero-profit) sets of policies. Secondly, they must choose policies which prevent new firms from entering and making positive profits.

In the case of a Nash equilibrium, where there is no foresight by existing firms, all equilibrium policies *must* be actuarially fair, whether or not consumers misperceive the probabilities of risks. As we shall see, the region of stability will be determined by the perceived expected utility of individuals, in each of the different risk classes. For the case of a Wilson equilibrium, where firms are assumed to have a special type of foresight, optimal policies are determined by the *perceived* expected utility of individuals. The degree of cross-subsidization between individuals will thus be a function of the misperceptions of the probabilities of a loss. We will illustrate how these two basic principles of a stable equilibrium apply to each of the cases discussed in the paper.

For ease of exposition and graphical convenience we develop our analysis in the following sections by assuming that there are only two risk classes – high and low – each of which face the same loss X.[3] The section below spells out the appropriate definitions and assumptions. We then briefly review the case where consumers have correct perceptions of the probability of a loss, in order to contrast the Nash and Wilson equilibria. These results also serve as a useful benchmark for investigating the problem of consumer misperceptions. Generalizations of these results to n risk groups and their welfare implications are discussed in the final section.

DEFINITIONS AND ASSUMPTIONS

Our simplified world consists of N consumers divided into high (H) and low (L) risk groups of sizes N_H and N_L, respectively. Each consumer faces a risk involving a potential loss (X) which he correctly estimates.[4]

Each group $i = H$, L has their own perception of the probability of a loss (φ_i) which may differ from the true probability (Φ_i). Neither X nor the φ_i can be influenced by consumer actions, so moral hazard problems do not exist. The initial wealth of consumers in the high and low-risk groups is given by W_H and W_L, respectively. Unless otherwise specified we assume $W_H = W_L = W$. If a loss does not occur, then the wealth level of group i is given by W_1; a loss results in wealth level of W_2. An uninsured individual in group i with perfect information on the probability of X thus faces a lottery yielding outcomes $W_1 = W_i$ and $W_2 = W_i - X$ with probabilities $1 - \Phi_i$ and Φ_i respectively.

The insurance industry consists of n identical firms which offer different insurance policies to consumers. Each firm is unable to distinguish between low and high-risk consumers who express an interest in purchasing insurance. Since we are interested in the stability conditions of equilibrium it is irrelevant whether firms have a correct perception of Φ_i. Equilibrium insurance policies reflect the condition of zero expected profits for each firm, so that the true probabilities of a loss will reveal themselves through a long-run adjustment policy.[5] Each policy j consists of a premium per dollar (p_j) and a specified amount of coverage (Q_j) which we denote by $\langle p_j, Q_j \rangle$. If a policy is only offered to group i because the firm can differentiate between consumers, then it is denoted by $\langle p_j^i, Q_j^i \rangle$. We are assuming that consumers are not allowed to purchase more than X dollars of insurance[6] and that claims are monitored to enforce this restriction. A consumer in group i selects from among the insurance policies offered him the one which maximizes his expected utility $[E(U_i)]$ where U_i is a von Neuman–Morgenstern utility function. We assume $U_i' > 0$, $U_i'' < 0$ so consumers are risk averse. If a person chooses policy $\langle p_j, Q_j \rangle$ based on the perceived probability φ_i, then his *ex ante* perceived utility is

$$E[U_i(\varphi_i)] = (1 - \varphi_i)U_i[W_i - p_jQ_j] + \varphi_iU_i[W_i - X + (1 - p_j)Q_j] \quad (4.1)$$

In measuring consumer welfare, we will be careful to distinguish between perceived and actual welfare, depending on whether φ_i or Φ_i is used in computing $E[U_i]$ in equation (4.1).

The primary interest of this study is on the impact of imperfect information on the stability of equilibrium and the welfare implications of alternative regulatory measures. In the next sections we will address the following questions with respect to the case where consumers correctly estimate Φ_i and the case where they misperceive these probabilities (that is, $\varphi_i \neq \Phi_i$).

(1) What are the relevant conditions with respect to (a) true and perceived probabilities of a loss, and (b) number of consumers in the high and low risk groups which lead to a stable Nash equilibrium?
(2) What are the characteristics of a Wilson equilibrium and how does it compare to a Nash equilibrium if it exists?
(3) What are the welfare implications of consumer misperceptions as these impact on own-group welfare and on other-group welfare at the market (Nash–Wilson) equilibrium?

CORRECT PERCEPTIONS BY CONSUMERS

Our analysis of resulting equilibrium with correct and incorrect perceptions of Φ by consumers will parallel the graphical methods introduced by R–S. They note that the implications of any insurance policies offered in the market can be reflected by their impact on consumer wealth in the two relevant states: no loss and loss. Denote by (W_1, W_2) consumer wealth in these two states, respectively. If $\langle p, Q \rangle$ were an insurance policy offered to either consumer group, then the representation of this policy in (W_1, W_2) space is seen from equation (4.1) to be

$$W_1 = W - pQ \quad \text{and} \quad W_2 = W - X + (1-p)Q \qquad (4.2)$$

Similarly, any point in (W_1, W_2) space corresponds to an insurance policy which might be marketed. Consumer decisions regarding the choice between insurance policies will be determined by maximizing their expected utility, so that the traditional iso-utility curve analysis applies.

PROPERTIES OF A NASH EQUILIBRIUM

Since firms cannot differentiate between high and low-risk consumers, then adverse selection problems may arise and a market equilibrium may or may not exist. R–S first show that no single policy (that is, pooled) equilibrium can exist. They then discuss conditions under which a separating Nash equilibrium, consisting of two policies $\langle p_H, Q_H \rangle$ and $\langle p_L, Q_L \rangle$ can exist. Two conditions are necessary. First, high-risk consumers must be offered full insurance at actuarial rates $\langle \Phi_H, X \rangle$; second, low-risk consumers must be offered an actuarially fair policy $\langle \Phi_L, Q_L \rangle$ whose utility to the high-risk consumers is identical to the policy $\langle \Phi_H, X \rangle$. In this case there is no incentive for the high-risk group to purchase a low-risk policy (which would create negative profits for firms). The resulting (potential) equilibrium is shown as α_H, α_L in Figure 4.1. These conditions are equivalent to having the firm maximize expected utility of the low-risk consumer while ensuring that there is no incentive for a high risk individual to buy a policy offered to a low-risk consumer. Hence, they conform to the basic principles for an equilibrium outlined in the Introduction. To see whether α_H, α_L is actually a stable Nash equilibrium, we must consider whether new entrants can make a positive profit if all firms continue to offer the above two policies. We first construct the market fair odds for pooled policies (that is, EF in Figure 4.1). Since there are N_H and N_L consumers in each risk class, the slope of this line is given by $-(1-\Phi)/\Phi$, where

$$\Phi = \frac{N_H \Phi_H + N_L \Phi_L}{N_H + N_L} = \frac{\Phi_H + R\Phi_L}{1 + R} \tag{4.3}$$

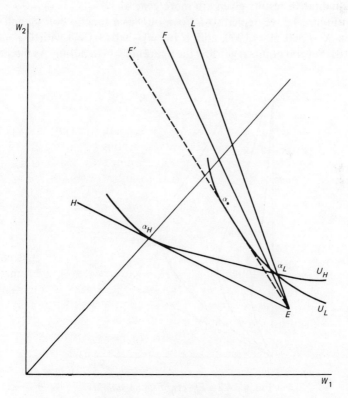

FIGURE 4.1 *Nash equilibrium*

and $R = N_L/N_H$. We then determine whether the iso-utility line, U_L, which passes through α_L allows a point such as α in Figure 4.1 above it and below the fair market odds line. If such a point exists, some enterprising new firm will make positive profits by offering this policy to consumers. This point is preferred by all consumers to both α_H and α_L. Whether or not such a point exists depends on the ratio of low to high-risk consumers in the market (that is, on R in equation (4.3)). As R decreases, the market odds line EF moves in the direction of EH and the area of instability decreases. Of interest is the maximal R, denoted by R^*, for which the separating equilibrium α_H, α_L is stable. In Figure 4.1 this would be the R corresponding to the market fair odds line EF' which is tangent to U_L.

To set the stage for our analysis of equilibrium when consumers have imperfect information and as a matter of interest in its own right, we consider a few examples illustrating how R^* varies as objective data changes. To be concrete we use the exponential utility function, although the qualitative results given are more general.

In Figure 4.2 we depict iso-R^* contours as a function of Φ_H and Φ_L when $X = 500$, $W = 1000$, and $U_i(w) = -\exp(-C_i w)$ with $C_H = C_L = 0.01$. Several points regarding the figure are worth noting. As the value

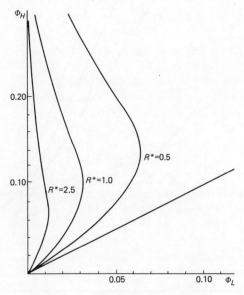

FIGURE 4.2   *Effects of Φ_i on stability*

of Φ_L increases, the maximum value of R^* at which the Nash equilibrium is stable decreases. For example, if $\Phi_H = 0.05$ and $\Phi_L = 0.01$ then $R^* = 2.59$; when $\Phi_H = 0.05$ and $\Phi_L = 0.03$ then R^* decreases to 0.63. The same pattern occurs along any ray $\{(\Phi_H, \Phi_L)/\Phi_H = t\Phi_L, t > 1\}$.

For Φ_H the situation is a bit more complicated. For any given Φ_L the value of R^* increases to a critical value as Φ_H increases and thereafter R^* decreases. The analysis of Figure 4.2 thus operationalizes the conjectures of R–S concerning the effects of Φ_i on the stability of equilibrium, while at the same time demonstrating that no simple conclusions regarding differences between Φ_H and Φ_L and resulting stability emerge.

Changes in risk aversion also affect stability. As the consumer becomes more risk averse he is willing to give up more W_1 for the same increase in W_2. Thus as the high-risk consumer becomes more risk averse the curve U_H becomes less steep so that α_L moves up on the fair odds line EL in Figure 4.1. This increases the region of stability. On the other hand, an increase in C_L causes U_L to become less steep which decreases the region of stability. A similar analysis can be undertaken with respect to the affect of changes in the loss X on stability. Higher losses reduce stability because the uninsured point E in Figure 4.1 is shifted downward with . consequent downward shifts in α_H and α_L.

Properties of a Wilson Equilibrium

When a separating, Nash equilibrium does not exist, one may argue (as do R–S) that the market is likely to fail in the absence of regulation. Alternatively, one may proceed as in Wilson (1977) and Spence (1978) to analyze competitive equilibrium by assuming a stronger equilibrium concept, one which attributes foresight and restraint to firms. Such assumptions raise a number of empirical questions which we will not pursue here. We will simply point out the implications of these alternative Nash–Wilson assumptions for the resulting market adjustment processes and equilibria.

In a traditional Nash equilibrium, each firm (including potential entrants) is assumed to determine the set of policies by maximizing its expected profits under the assumption that all other firms make no changes in their current offerings. In the Wilson equilibrium, each firm determines its optimal set of policy offerings under the assumption that any currently marketed policies which become unprofitable as a result of their new offerings will no longer be offered in the marketplace. Clearly, if a Nash equilibrium exists it is also a Wilson equilibrium.

Figure 4.3 depicts a case where a stable separating (Nash) equilibrium does not exist. A Wilson equilibrium will, nonetheless, always exist for this case (as Miyasaki, 1977, proved). Following Dahlby (1981), the construction of the Wilson equilibrium proceeds as follows. First, the dotted line CD in the Figure is constructed as follows. To each point on BD, like X, the unique point Y on the high-risk iso-utility contour U_H^1 passing through X is determined for which the policies X and Y together achieve zero profits when the high-risk consumers buy X and the low-risk consumers buy Y. Thus, the dotted line CD is the locus of low-risk policies necessary to achieve zero profits if high-risk consumers are offered full insurance. It can then be verified (see Spence, 1978) that the Wilson equilibrium is the pair of policies $\alpha^\omega = (\alpha_H^\omega, \alpha_L^\omega)$, illustrated in Figure 4.3, where the low-risk consumer maximizes his expected utility along CD. The logic establishing that α^ω is indeed a Wilson equilibrium is

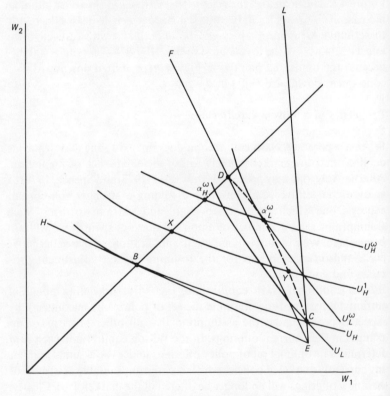

FIGURE 4.3 *Wilson equilibrium*

that the only way for a firm to possibly make profits on a policy deviating from α^ω is if all remaining firms continue to offer α^ω, suffering losses in the process. Given the Wilson assumptions, the deviant policy would never be offered in the first place. The resulting equilibrium α^ω turns out to be unique (see M–S–D). As is apparent from Figure 4.3, a Wilson equilibrium always involves subsidies from low-risk to high-risk consumers whenever it does not coincide with the Nash equilibrium.

MISPERCEPTIONS BY CONSUMERS

In this section we will develop equilibrium results for the case where consumers misperceive the probability of a loss, assuming it to be $\varphi_i \neq \Phi_i$. To motivate the analysis and to provide a contrast with the previous section we will first look at the case where firms have perfect knowledge of the risk facing each of their customers so that they do not have adverse selection problems and a Nash equilibrium exists. We will then turn to the case where firms cannot distinguish between high and low-risk customers, still maintaining the assumption that either or both groups of insured misperceives the probability of a loss.

Perfect Information by Firms

Suppose consumers misperceive Φ_i, believing it to be φ_i; firms continue to have perfect information on Φ_i. Hence the consumer's iso-utility curves are based on φ_i instead of Φ_i. Two cases are possible: either $\varphi_i > \Phi_i$ or $\varphi_i < \Phi_i$. We depict both of these situations in Figure 4.4. Let us concentrate first on the high risk group. Suppose that a consumer estimates $\varphi_H = \varphi_H^1 > \Phi_H$. He is then willing to purchase full insurance (for example, the policy λ) at more than the actuarially fair price as shown by the perceived iso-utility curve U_H^1. This curve is tangent to the consumer's perceived odds line, EH_1, which is below EH because $\varphi_H > \Phi_H$.[7] Firms offering the policy λ would make positive profits, thus inducing entry by others at a lower premium. Price will continue to fall until it reaches an equilibrium at α_H.

If consumers underestimate the risk so that $\varphi_H = \varphi_H^2 < \Phi_H$ their perceived odds line, EH_2, is above EH. They will only want to purchase full coverage if $p_H = \varphi_H < \Phi_H$. Firms offering such a policy will thus lose money, so that equilibrium will be established at the point where the consumer's perceived iso-utility curve, U_H^2, is tangent to the objective fair odds line EH. This point α_H^2 indicates that the resulting market

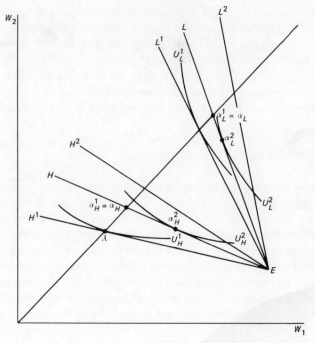

FIGURE 4.4   *Equilibrium under consumer misperceptions*

equilibrium will provide a policy with less than full coverage when firms
have perfect information and consumers underestimate Φ_H. The
analogous situation holds for low-risk consumers who underestimate
their risk as shown by the equilibrium point α_2^L in Figure 4.4.

To illustrate the impact of consumer misperception on equilibrium
consider an example using an exponential function $U_1 = -b\exp{(C_iw)}$
where C_i is the risk aversion coefficient. The relevant objective data are

$$\Phi_H = 0.04; \quad \Phi_H = 0.02; \quad X = 500; \quad W = 1000$$

The equilibrium insurance policies are

$$\langle p_H, Q_H \rangle = \langle 0.04, 500 \rangle; \quad \langle p_L, Q_L \rangle = \langle 0.02, 500 \rangle$$

if consumers have perfect information. In this case α_H and α_L are
respectively (980, 980) and (990, 990) no matter how risk averse any
individual may be. To examine the impact of misperception on

TABLE 4.1 *The effects of consumer misperceptions*

Consumer perceptions	Objective data			
	$\Phi_H = 0.04$ $C_H = 00.1$ α_H	$\Phi_H = 0.02$ $C_H = 0.02$ α_H	$X = 500$ $C_L = 0.01$ α_L	$W = 1000$ $C_L = 0.02$ α_L
$\phi_H \geqslant \Phi_H$	(980.0, 980.0)	(980.0, 980.0)	–	–
$\phi_L \geqslant \Phi_L$	–	–	(990.0, 990.0)	(990.0, 990.0)
$\phi_H = 0.03$	(981.2, 951.2)	(980.6, 965.2)	–	–
$\phi_L = 0.01$	–	–	(991.4, 921.4)	(990.7, 955.7)

equilibrium values it is instructive to vary not only φ_H and φ_L but also C_H and C_L. Table 4.1 presents illustrative results. The first row represents the case where probabilities are either known perfectly or overestimated. The equilibrium policy is always full insurance. When probabilities are underestimated the equilibrium policy will deviate increasingly from full insurance as the consumer becomes less risk averse. For example, if $\varphi_L = 0.01$ and $C_L = 0.02$ then $\alpha_H = (990.7, 955.7)$ compared with $\alpha_H = (991.4, 921.4)$ when $C_L = 0.01$.

We close this section by noting that the above analysis goes through unchanged if consumers also misestimate the magnitude of the loss X. In this case, their estimate of X, say X_i for group i, replaces X in equation (4.1) in computing perceived expected utility. Under- (over)estimates of X then have the same effect on perceived iso-expected utility contours and resulting market equilibrium as under- (over)estimates of Φ.

Imperfect Information by Firms

Suppose that firms cannot distinguish between high- and low-risk consumers, and that consumers may misperceive the probability of a loss. Just as we proceeded with informed firms (see Figure 4.4), so here too the only change required to incorporate consumer misperceptions into the analysis of the previous section is to substitute *perceived* for *actual* expected utility contours in the analysis. We restrict our attention here to misperceptions of Φ, although a similar analysis applies for misperceptions of X, as discussed just above.

Nash Equilibrium

We illustrate in Figure 4.5 the process for determining the Nash separating equilibrium if it exists. Of fundamental concern to us are the effects of misinformation on market stability and the resulting equilibrium policies. It is relatively straightforward to determine what impact deviations of φ_H and φ_L from the true parameters will have on these characteristics. In the case of the high risk group we note that if $\varphi_H > \Phi_H$ then full coverage will be offered. Furthermore as Φ_H increases, the point α_L moves up the fair odds line EL and increases the region of stability. We illustrate these points in Figure 4.5 by constructing two iso-utility curves U_H^1, U_H^2 which correspond to $\varphi_H^1 > \Phi_H$ and $\Phi_H^2 < \Phi_H$, respectively. If all other data remain constant, then we see that the policies $\{\alpha_H^1, \alpha_L^1\}$ associated with φ_H^1 will be stable. On the other hand, the policy $\{\alpha_H^2, \alpha_L^2\}$ is unstable because U_L^2 is below the market fair odds line EF,

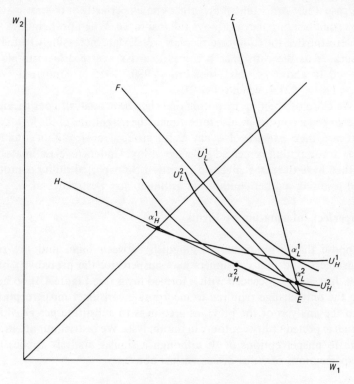

FIGURE 4.5 *Illustrating the effects of misperceptions of Φ_H*

thus enabling a new firm to enter and make positive profits in the short-run. Note that we can generate similar effects on stability by changing the high-risk consumer's risk aversion: increasing the degree of risk aversion produces the same effect as increasing φ_H.

Misperception by low-risk consumers is illustrated in Figure 4.6 for the case where $\varphi_H = \Phi_H$. It should be noted that α_L will not be affected by misperception on the part of the low-risk consumer because it is determined solely by the high-risk iso-utility curve associated with α_H, in this case U_H. If low-risk consumers overestimate Φ_L (that is, $\varphi_L^1 > \Phi_L$) then the iso-utility curve is given by U_L^1. The curve U_L^2 represents the case where $\varphi_L^2 < \Phi_L$. In general, the region of stability is increased as φ_L decreases. In Figure 4.6 a stable separating equilibrium exists when $\varphi_L = \varphi_L^2$ but not when $\varphi_L = \varphi_L^1 > \varphi_L^2$. The impact of misperception of Φ_L produces similar effects in stability as changes in risk aversion. As the consumer becomes more risk averse his iso-utility curve become less steep reflecting a willingness to sacrifice more W_1 for the same amount of W_2. This is similar to the effects just discussed for increases in φ_L.

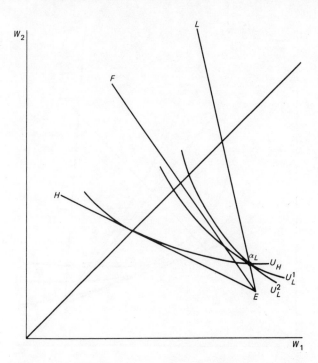

FIGURE 4.6   *Illustrating the effects of misperceptions of* Φ_L

The above illustrative examples assumed that all consumers in the high and low-risk groups had the same misestimates of the probability. If there were a whole spectrum of misestimates then the procedure for determining whether a stable equilibrium exists is based on similar principles. There would be a range of policies offered to high-risk individuals ranging from full coverage for all those who perceive $\varphi_H \geq \Phi_H$ to the lowest tangency of the U_H curve to the fair odds line. Figure 4.7 depicts the three policies α_1^H, α_2^H, α_3^H, for the case where two high-risk groups (2 and 3) underestimate Φ_H and one (group 1) correctly estimates it. There is only one policy for the low-risk group – α_3^L which is determined by the intersection of U_3^H with EL. This construction guarantees that every high-risk consumer is provided a policy which maximizes his perceived expected utility at actuarial rates (that is, along EH), and all low-risk consumers are offered the highest coverage which, at actuarial rates (along EL), is consistent with not attracting any high-risk consumers to the policy intended for low-risk consumers.

We thus see that low-risk individuals are penalized by those high risk

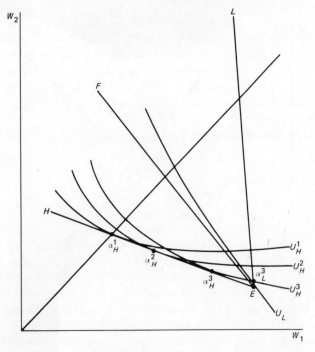

FIGURE 4.7 *Nash equilibrium with consumer misperceptions*

consumers underestimating φ_H – they are offered less coverage than if they had estimated $\varphi_H = \Phi_H$. The stability of equilibrium is determined by looking at the position of the *lowest* U_L curve (that is, the U_L curve corresponding to the minimum φ_L) to the fair odds line. The situation least likely to lead to stability is if some high-risk consumers grossly underestimate Φ_H and some low-risk consumers overestimate Φ_L. It should now be clear why stability of Nash equilibrium is so sensitive to perceptions of Φ_i by consumers. Suppose low-risk consumers estimate $\varphi_L \gg \Phi_L$ and one high risk consumer estimates $\varphi_H \ll \Phi_H$. What otherwise may have been a stable Nash equilibrium is now unstable. This observation suggests that the existence of a Nash equilibrium can be sensitive to consumer (mis)perceptions of the risk involved.[8]

Wilson Equilibrium

As we will see, the Wilson equilibrium behaves somewhat more smoothly in response to consumer misperceptions. The procedure for determining the Wilson equilibrium set of policies parallels the one described above for the Nash equilibrium. In particular, $\varphi_H^{\min}$ is the lowest estimate of Φ_H by high-risk individuals and $\varphi_H^{\max}$ is the highest estimate of Φ_L by the low-risk individuals, then the set of optimal policies for all individuals is based on these two extreme groups just as in the Nash equilibrium case. The one critical difference between the two cases is that in a Nash equilibrium there are no cross-subsidies, whereas the Wilson equilibrium entails such subsidies just as in the case where consumer perceptions are accurate.

We restrict our attention here to deriving the Wilson equilibrium when there are just four groups,[9] denoted H_1, H_2, L_1, L_2, where

$$\varphi_H^1 \geq \Phi_H > \varphi_H^2; \quad \varphi_L^1 \geq \Phi_L > \varphi_L^2$$

Thus, groups $\{H_1, L_1\}$ overestimate and groups $\{H_2, L_2\}$ underestimate their respective accident probabilities. Our first concern will be to determine, for any fixed level of total subsidy from low- to high-risk consumers, what high-risk policies can be offered in the market. Thereafter we analyze what level of subsidy is compatible with market equilibrium under the Wilson assumptions on firm adjustment.

We begin by noting that if a subsidy is provided any high-risk group, then it must be provided in such a manner that the *perceived* expected utility of the group in question is maximized over all policies offering the same level of subsidy. Otherwise a new entrant could offer the group a policy it would prefer and which would entail a lower subsidy. Now the set of all constant-subsidy policies for the high-risk group is easily represented in (W_1, W_2) space by the transformation

$$(W_1, W_2) \to (W_1 + S, W_2 + S)$$

where S is the subsidy involved. In Figure 4.8, the parallel lines S_0, S_1, S_2 indicate sets of policies with increasing levels of subsidy to the high-risk group, where S_0, the zero-subsidy line, is just the fair odds line for the high-risk group.

The condition that perceived expected utility be maximized for each high-risk sub-group along the iso-subsidy lines just derived is reflected in Figure 4.8. For group 2 this yields the locus $\mathscr{L}_H^2$ which is the set of policies obtained through the tangency of the iso-perceived utility contours to the iso-subsidy lines. For group 1, the maximizing policy along any iso-

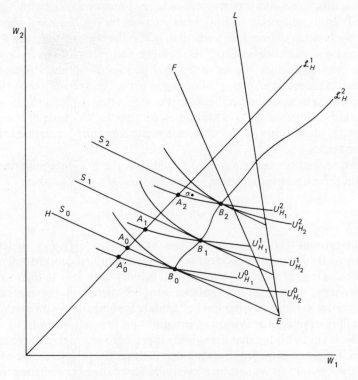

FIGURE 4.8   *Constructing a Wilson equilibrium*

subsidy line is just the full-insurance policy since all our consumers are risk averse and φ_H^1 is no smaller than Φ_H.

Now what we have noted above is that only policies on $\mathscr{L}_H^1$ or $\mathscr{L}_H^2$ can be offered to groups 1 and 2, respectively. A further feasibility restriction is that whatever is offered to group 2 must not be preferred by group 1 to the policy intended for them. For example, suppose the policies (A_1, B_2) in Figure 4.8 were offered on the market. Clearly *all* of the high-risk consumers would prefer B_2 to the policy A_1. A new entrant could then offer the policy α and attract only individuals from group 1. Such a new entrant would thus pay the high-risk group as a whole a smaller subsidy. Thus, if B_2 is to be offered at all, competition (to minimize total subsidies to the high-risk group) will push the solution to the pair (A_2, B_2). A similar argument holds for the pair (A_1, B_1). Note for (A_0, B_0), however, that the point A_0', if offered, would offer positive profits, thus inducing entry and pushing the solution to (A_0, B_0).

We see from the above discussion that only policies (α_H^1, α_H^2) satisfying the following conditions can qualify as candidates for the policies offered to the high-risk groups: first, each of the α_H^i must belong to the respective perceived utility maximizing curve $\mathscr{L}_H^i$: and secondly, the condition

$$E[U_H^1(\alpha_H^1)] = E[U_H^1(\alpha_H^2)]$$

must obtain unless this implies a positive subsidy to group 1, in which case group 1 is offered the actuarially fair, full-coverage policy.

We note that the above procedure provides us, for any pre-specified subsidy S to the high-risk group, with a unique pair of policies $\langle \alpha_H^1(S), \alpha_H^2(S) \rangle$ which can be marketed to these two high-risk groups.

Having determined feasible policy offerings for the high-risk groups for any specified subsidy level S, we can now proceed to determine the amount of subsidy to the high-risk groups which is compatible with a Wilson equilibrium. We proceed as in Figure 4.3 to construct a locus of low-risk policies which, if purchased together with the pair $\langle \alpha_H^1(S), \alpha_H^2(S) \rangle$, will provide a subsidy of S to the high-risk groups and are such that no one in the high-risk group finds it attractive to switch to the policy intended for the low-risk groups. Figure 4.9 summarizes this process, paralleling that described in Figure 4.3. As before, the desired locus of low-risk policies is labelled CD. Thus, the policies (A_i, B_i, C_i), $i = 0, 1, 2$, are constructed so that (a) zero profits are achieved, (b) at the level of subsidy implied for each high-risk group the utility of that group is maximized, and (c) no one prefers the policy intended for any other group to his own.

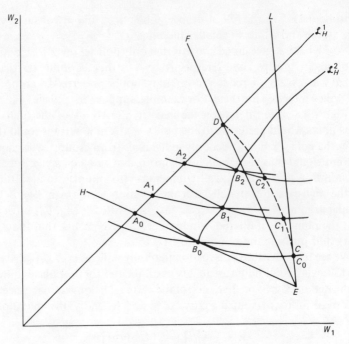

FIGURE 4.9   *Constructing zero-profit policy bundles*

The final piece of the Wilson equilibrium puzzle can now be put into place, namely the determination of the particular policy (there will only be one) offered to the low-risk group. Just as in Figure 4.3, it is easy to see that the policy offered to the low-risk group must be such as to maximize their welfare along the zero-profits contour CD in Figure 4.9. Moreover, since the low-risk group with the highest misperception will be the easiest to skim off, it must in fact be this group whose perceived utility is maximized along CD. Putting all of this together we obtain the Wilson equilibrium depicted in Figure 4.10 as the policy $\langle \alpha_H^1, \alpha_H^2, \alpha_L \rangle$.

We may note immediately that as the maximal overestimate of any low-risk group increases (that is, as α_L^i increases), the Wilson equilibrium moves up the zero profit contour CD. Thus, the policy α_L' might correspond to the Wilson equilibrium policy offered to all low-risk consumers if φ_L^1 were to increase (or if there were another sub-group within the low-risk group with higher overestimates of Φ_L than those of sub-group L_1). Thus, overestimates by any sub-group in the low-risk group costs everyone in the low-risk group additional taxes which flow to the high-risk group as subsidies.

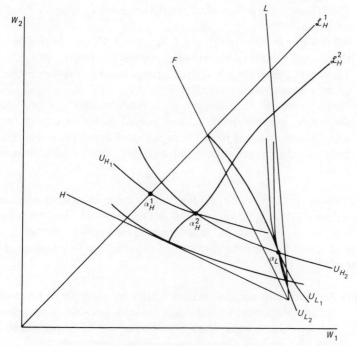

FIGURE 4.10 *Wilson equilibrium*

Similarly, a more pronounced underestimation by the high-risk group reduces the amount of coverage low-risk groups are offered in equilibrium. Thus, we see that information imperfections on the part of consumers can affect both welfare outcomes associated with market equilibrium as well as the nature and existence of such equilibria.

GENERALIZATIONS AND WELFARE IMPLICATIONS

The graphical procedure described above for investigating stability of Nash equilibrium and characterizing Wilson equilibria is quite general. If there are n different risk groups and a range of misperceptions within each one of these groups the same general principles above apply.

(1) There can be multiple policies offered to the highest risk group (denoted H) depending on the extent of their misperceptions.

(2) There is only one policy offered to the lowest risk group (denoted L) based on $\varphi_L^{\max}$.

(3) All risk groups between H and L have their policies determined so that an individual in a higher risk group has *no* incentive to purchase a policy designed for a lower risk group. Naturally this incentive is based on perceived expected utility.

(4) With respect to the stability of a Nash equilibrium one must determine whether there is any pooled policy which is more attractive to adjacent paired groups than the proposed separating policies and at the same time yields a profit to any firm offering such a policy.

The above principles are studied analytically in Kleindorfer and Kunreuther (1981) following the M–S–D framework. Assuming their validity for the moment, the following welfare implications, which we have analyzed here for the case of two groups, may be conjectured in general.

(W1) An increasing underestimation of risk by the higher risk groups reduces the amount of coverage low-risk individuals are offered (under either a stable Nash equilibrium or a Wilson equilibrium) and also reduces the (*ex ante* objective) expected utility of the resulting policy offered to low-risk individuals.

(W2) Increasing overestimation of risk by the lower risk groups increases the tax paid by these low-risk people because they demand more insurance.

Besides verifying (W1) and (W2) generally, several additional welfare and regulatory matters are of interest. For example, when is compulsory insurance a welfare-improving regulation?[10] How is learning incorporated into both firms' knowledge of consumers as well as consumers' knowledge of the risks against which they are insuring themselves. Finally, and perhaps most importantly, there is the question of the applicability of the price-quantity framework we have been using here.

In contrast with the price-quantity framework, one might suppose that insurance policies are specified through a premium (price per dollar of coverage) as in Pauly (1974) and Kunreuther and Pauly (1981), where each customer then determines the total coverage he or she will purchase at the stated premium. The primary reason why such pricing policies may be a better model of actual insurance markets than price-quality policies was already recognized by R–S, viz. price-quantity policies require a central monitoring system for the entire insurance industry if they are to function. If, for example, a policy $\langle p, Q \rangle$ is offered with $p < \Phi_H$ and $Q < X$, then high-risk consumers would buy several such policies (with total coverage approximating X) from different firms, thus undermining the intended self-selection mechanism inherent in offering less than full coverage. The only way to prevent this is to monitor all (high-risk) consumer purchases to ensure that only one policy is purchased. Such a central monitoring system is problematical in a competitive market. Moreover, if such a monitoring system could be set up at low cost, it is also likely that, at little additional cost, sophisticated statistical techniques could be used to classify customers over time according to their risk class. Each customer could then be offered the socially optimal policy of full coverage at actuarial rates.

The broader issue here is the empirical question of which forms of policy are actually offered to the consumer in various insurance contexts as well as how firms and consumers gather and process information relating to these policies. This issue has both institutional as well as decision theoretic characteristics (for example, involving insurance agents' behavior in representing available policies). As we have seen in this chapter, informational and behavioral differences resulting from the mutual interaction of firms and consumers have interesting implications for market equilibrium, regulation and welfare.

NOTES

1. The research in this paper is supported by NSF Grant No. 5–22669 and in part by the Bundesministerium fuer Forschung und Technologie, FRG, contract no. 321/7591/RGB 8001. While support for this work is gratefully acknowledged, the views expressed are the authors' and not necessarily shared by the sponsor. The authors would also like to express their appreciation to Uday Apte for his computational assistance and to Michael Rothschild and Joseph Stiglitz, and the participants in the Conference on the Economics of Regulation in Berlin, for their helpful comments on an earlier draft.
2. The results derived below also hold if the Q_j are interpreted as maximum or minimum coverage limits and are allowed to vary according to the premium.
3. The analyses by R–S, Wilson, Miyasaki and Dahlby all make these same assumptions.
4. The case where consumers misestimate X is also discussed briefly below and turns out to be analogous to the case where consumers misestimate Φ. We thank Robert Willig for raising this point.
5. Firms' possible misperceptions of probabilities (or losses) do become important in analyzing the dynamics of the industry adjustment process in attaining equilibrium.
6. This assumption is not critical for our analysis. For example, if consumers estimate $Q_H > \Phi_H$ and firms offer actuarially fair premiums then consumers will purchase $Q_H > X$ if such a policy were offered.

7. Iso-utility contours of the perceived utility function $E[(U)] = (1-\varphi)U(W_1) + \varphi U(W_2)$ are all tangent to the perceived fair odds line $W_2 = -[(1-\varphi)/\varphi]W_1 + (W/\varphi) - X$ where full coverage occurs (that is, where $W_1 = W_2$). The proof follows by implicit differentiation of the iso-utility contours along the full-insurance line $W_1 = W_2$.
8. Of course, we assume away fixed costs of entry in this perfectly competitive model. If these were present, they would naturally dampen the entry threat to existing firms resulting from changes of the above sort, where only one (or a few) high-risk consumers' perceptions changed.
9. A more formal derivation for multiple sub-groups is contained in Kleindorfer and Kunreuther (1981).
10. See Dahlby (1981) for an analysis of this question when consumers are perfectly informed.

REFERENCES

Arrow, K. (1963) 'Uncertainty and the Welfare Economics of Medical Care'. *American Economic Review*, 53, 941–73.
Dahlby, B. (1981) 'Adverse Selection and Pareto Improvements Through Compulsory Insurance', vol. 37, no. 3, pp. 547–58.
Fischhoff, B., P. Slovic and S. Lichtenstein (1978) 'Fault Trees: Sensitivity of Estimated Failure Probabilities to Problem Representation', *Journal of Experimental Psychology: Human Perception Performance*, 4, 330–44.
Finsinger, J. (1983) 'Competition, Ownership, and Control in Markets with Imperfect Information: The Case of the German Liability and Life Insurance Markets.' (in this volume).
Kleindorfer, P. R. and H. Kunreuther (1981) 'Consumer Misperceptions and Equilibrium in Insurance Markets', (mimeo).
Kunreuther, H. R. Ginsberg, L. Miller, P. Sagi, P. Slovic, B. Borkan and N. Katz (1978) *Disaster Insurance Protection: Public Policy Lessons*, (New York: Wiley Interscience, 1978).
Kunreuther, H., and M. Pauly (1981) 'Equilibrium in Insurance Markets with Experience Rating', IIM Proceedings, Berlin (West), July.
Miyasaki, H. (1977) 'The rat race and internal labor markets', *The Bell Journal of Economics*, 8, 394–418.
Pauly, M. (1974) 'Over Insurance and Public Provision of Insurance: The Roles of Moral Hazard and Adverse Selection', *Quarterly Journal of Economics*, 88, 44–62.
Rothschild, M. and J. Stiglitz (1976) 'Equilibrium in Competitive Insurance Markets: An Essay in the Economics of Imperfect Information', *Quarterly Journal of Economics*, 90, 629–49.
Spence, M. (1978) 'Product Differentiation and Consumer Choice in Insurance Markets', *Journal of Public Economics*, 10, 427–47.
Williamson, O. (1975) *Markets and Hierarchies* (New York: The Free Press, 1975).
Wilson, C. (1977). A Model of Insurance Markets with Incomplete Information', *Journal of Economic Theory*, 16, 167–207.

5 Equilibrium in Insurance Markets with Experience Rating

HOWARD KUNREUTHER and MARK PAULY[1]

INTRODUCTION

This chapter investigates the functioning of insurance markets in which insurers can obtain specific and private knowledge of the characteristics of their customers. In particular, we focus on the case where the insurer obtains 'inside information' by observing the loss experience of its customers and utilizes these data to charge differential premiums. This type of 'experience rating' of individuals or groups is commonly used by firms in setting rates for automobile, health, and unemployment insurance.

The following problem is analyzed in detail. Suppose that a set of customers has been with a specific insurance firm for t years during which time the firm has collected information on their claims experience and these data are not available to others. Not having direct knowledge of each customer's risk class, the insurance firm utilizes claims data to set premiums. What schedule of rates should be set so that no customer will have an incentive to purchase insurance elsewhere in period $t + 1$? We show that the resulting premium schedule leads to an equilibrium in which monopoly profits are earned even if entry by new firms into the insurance market is perfectly free. We refer to this solution as a *single-period equilibrium* since firms can change their price from one period to the next and customers are free to stay or leave as they see fit. Regulation of premiums and profits may be appropriate for this situation even though firms based their rates on customers' past experience.

91

The models we discuss are concerned with experience rating of individuals. While this type of rating occurs for some insurance (for example, automobile), for others experience rating applies mainly to groups (for example, health insurance). Our model also applies to groups if the quantity of insurance purchased is chosen in a way that minimizes its premium cost and if the 'group' knows its own risk composition.[2]

The existence and character of equilibrium in insurance markets with adverse selection has been dealt with by Rothschild and Stiglitz (hereafter referred to as R–S) (1976) and Pauly (1974). R–S suggest that firms will market insurance contracts which specify price and the total amount of insurance purchased to potential customers. The total quantity of coverage acts as a signal to differentiate the high and low risks. Pauly, in contrast, suggests that insurers cannot be expected to obtain accurate information on the total purchases of any individual, since it will be in the interest of the individual and a supplemental insurer to conceal the fact of purchase. Extensions of the R–S approach, using different concepts of static equilibrium, have been provided by Wilson (1977), Miyasaki (1977), Grossman (1979), and Spence (1978). Pauly's approach has been analyzed by Johnson (1978), Jaynes (1978) and Dahlby (1980).

In this chapter we make Pauly's assumption that firms do not know the total amount of insurance an individual has purchased. We do so for three reasons.

(1) The empirical support for the assumption that all firms do exchange information about total purchases of insurance is weak. While some firms exchange such information, the frequency of complaints about the failure of such 'coordination of benefits' schemes is legion (Follman 1963).
(2) If insurers do not have accurate information on total purchases then there is an incentive for individuals to purchase policies from several firms and conceal their portfolio. This type of behavior prevents any firm from marketing a set of 'price-quantity' policies since potential customers will always purchase the one with the lowest cost per dollar coverage.
(3) Suppose one accepts the R–S assumptions that firms can monitor total purchases and that insurance demand varies with risk class. Then the quantity of insurance bought by any customer is a perfect and instantaneous signal of the individual's risk category.[3]

The chapter is organized as follows. We first begin by considering a static model in which the firm currently selling insurance to an individual is fully informed about his risk class, while other potential insurers have no information about his risk class. In this 'end state' model, firm or consumer foresight is not relevant. We explore possible equilibrium concepts for such a model. The third section develops a model in which firms obtain information over time from the claims experience of the insured and uses this information in a Bayesian fashion to adjust individual premiums to experience. Firms also require non-negative profits in each period. We then examine the characteristics of this process of linked single-period equilibria. The final section draws out lessons for regulation policy and suggests possible applications and extensions of the analysis.

CURRENT SELLERS WITH PERFECT INFORMATION

Relevant Assumptions

Our world consists of two types of consumers each of whom faces a single loss (X) which is correctly estimated and which is uncorrelated between individuals. Each type i has a different probability of a loss, Φ_i, $i = H, L$ for the high and low risk groups respectively $(\Phi_H > \Phi_L)$. The consumers correctly perceive these values of Φ_i. The proportion of high and low risk consumers is given by N_H and N_L, respectively. Type i's preference is represented by a von Neumann–Morgenstern utility function, U_i, and it determines the optimal amount of insurance to purchase by maximizing expected utility $E(U_i)$.

The insurance industry consists of n firms, all of whom estimate X correctly. We assume that each consumer has been insured by the same firm for a sufficiently long period of time that the insurer has collected enough information through claim payments and other data to specify Φ_i exactly for each individual. The remaining $n - 1$ firms in the industry *cannot* determine whether individuals insured by others are high or low risk people. Each insurer offers a premium, P_i, to individuals in risk group i, without specifying the amount of coverage (Q_i) which has to be purhased except that $0 \leq Q_i \leq X$. If firms have information on the risk class of their clients they can charge differential premiums to high and low risk individuals; other firms in the industry are forced to charge the same premium to both groups because they cannot distinguish high risks from low risks.

We now characterize the strategies available to insurers and consider the possibility of equilibrium. With respect to a particular client it is useful to think of firms as either being 'informed', that is, having sold a policy to an individual in the previous period, or 'uninformed', that is, treating the client as a new customer. Consider first the situation of a representative uninformed firm. It knows that each consumer has the insurance demand curve

$$D_i = f(\Phi_i, P_i), \quad i = H, L \tag{5.1}$$

which is derived from constrained utility maximization. Since the uninformed firm cannot distinguish between risks, it will have to set $P_H = P_L = P$. In a free-entry world with firms that maximize expected profit, the equilibrium premium P^* would be given by the lowest value of P such that

$$E(\pi) = (P - \Phi_L)Q_L N_L + (P - \Phi_H)Q_H N_H = 0 \tag{5.2}$$

where Q_L is the total amount purchased by L's and Q_H is the total amount purchased by H's at the uniform premium P. Figure 5.1 illustrates the case of an equilibrium when both groups purchase insurance. The low risk group subsidizes the high risk group and purchases partial coverage $Q_L < X$ whenever $P^* > \Phi_L$, while the high risk individuals purchase full coverage, $Q_H = X$, at subsidized rates ($P^* < \Phi_H$).[4]

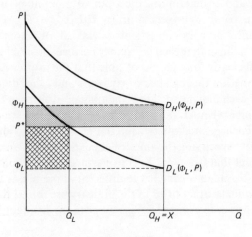

FIGURE 5.1

The informed insurer can use his exact knowledge of each present customer's Φ_i, $i = H, L$, to set rates tailored to each customer's experience. For high risk individuals, the informed firm will reduce its expected profits if it charges less than Φ_H. For low risk individuals, the rate it will charge will depend on the premium charged by uninformed firms. The informed firm maximizes expected profits by charging low risk individuals a little less than the price offered by the uninformed firm to all purchasers of insurance. (The uninformed firm's price must be larger than P^* for it to earn profits.) The informed firm then attracts all low risks, and makes profits of $(P_L^I - Q_L)N_L$, which rises as P_L^I rises. If uninformed firms are charging $P^* + \delta$, for example, the informed firm will want to charge its low risk customers the lower of one of two rates. It will either charge P^* or it will charge $\hat{P}_L$, the premium which would maximize profits on low-risk insureds if the firm were a monopolist. At the other extreme, if uninformed firms are charging Φ_H to everyone, then the informed firm will charge either $\Phi_H - \varepsilon$ or $\hat{P}_L$, whichever is less.

But just as the informed firm's optimal pricing strategy depends on the strategies selected by uninformed firms, so does an uninformed firm's strategy depend on what the informed firm is doing. The strategic combinations and payoffs are shown as the payoff matrix, in Figure 5.2, with the upper expression in each labelled cell 1–4 being the payoff (profits) to the informed firm (I), and the lower expression the payoffs to the uninformed firm (U). When one type of firm obtains no business, and

Uninformed firm Informed firm	$P^U = (P^* + \delta) < \Phi_H$	$P^U = \Phi_H$
$P_L^I = P^*$ $P_H^I = \Phi_H$	(1) $N_L Q_L (P^* - \Phi_L) > 0$ $N_H Q_H (P^* + \delta - \Phi_H) < 0$	(2) $N_L Q_L (P^* - \Phi_L) > 0$ 0
$P_L^I = \Phi_H - \varepsilon$ $P_H^I = \Phi_H$	(3) 0 $(N_L Q_L + N_H Q_H)(P^* + \delta) - N_L Q_L \Phi_L$ $- N_H Q_H \Phi_H > 0$	(4) $N_L Q_L (P_H - \varepsilon - \Phi_L) > 0$ 0

FIGURE 5.2 *Payoff matrix for informed and uninformed firms*

all customers purchase from the other type of firm, a profit level of zero is entered. Here we are assuming that both P^* and Φ_H are less than $\hat{P}_L$.[5]

Kunreuther and Pauly (1981) have shown that a stable equilibrium exists if one assumes the firms behave in a Stackelberg leader–follower mode. Specifically, the informed firm plays the role of leader and sets a price structure based on its old customers; the uninformed firm follows suit. The single period equilibrium is also stable if one assumes that firms follow a policy that maximizes the minimum profit they could attain no matter what uninformed firms do.

An Illustrative Example

A simple example illustrates how one determines a single period equilibrium for the above problem.[6] Risk averse consumers in each type i with wealth, A_i, want to choose a value of Q_i given Φ_i and P_i which maximizes $E[U_i(Q_i)]$. For this two state problem this is

$$E[U_i(Q_i)] = \Phi_i U_i[A_i + X - (1 - P_i)Q_i] + (1 - \Phi_i)U_i(A_i - P_iQ_i)$$
(5.3)

subject to

$$0 \leq Q_i \leq X$$

Let R_i be the contingency price ratio

$$\{P_i(1 - \Phi_i)\}/\{(1 - P_i)\Phi_i\}$$

and define $R_i^{\max}$ and $R_i^{\min}$ as the values of R_i where $Q_i = 0$ and $Q_i = X$, respectively, when one maximizes $E[U_i(Q_i)]$ without any constraint on Q_i. Then if consumers are risk averse so that $U_i' > 0$ and $U_i'' < 0$ the optimal solution to (4) is given by:

$$Q_i = 0 \quad \text{if} \quad R_i \geq R_i^{\max}$$
$$R_i = \frac{U_i'(A_i - P_iQ_i)}{U_i'\{A_i - X - (1 - P_i)Q_i\}} \quad \text{if} \quad R_i^{\min} < R_i < R_i^{\max} \qquad (5.4)$$
$$Q_i = X \quad \text{if} \quad R_i \leq R_i^{\min}$$

Whenever $P_i \leq \Phi_i$, then $Q_i = X$, since in this range the premium is either actuarially fair or subsidized. Suppose both consumer types have identical utility functions given by the exponential $U_H(Y) = U_L(Y) =$

$-\,\mathrm{e}^{-cY}$, where c is the risk aversion coefficient. Then Q_i is determined by

$$
\begin{array}{llll}
& Q_L = 0 & \text{if} & (\ln R_i) \geq cX \\
Q_L = X - (\ln R_i)/c & & \text{if} & \mathrm{e}^{cx} > R_i > 1 \\
& Q_L = X & \text{if} & R_i \leq 1
\end{array}
\tag{5.5}
$$

Figure 5.3 depicts the profit maximizing set of premiums for the specific case where $\Phi_H = 0.30$, $\Phi_L = 0.10$, $X = 40$, $c = 0.04$ and $N_H = N_L = 0.5$. Uninformed firms would be forced to charge both high and low risk customers $P^* = 0.254$. The informed firms maximize their profits by charging high risk customers $P_H^* = \Phi_H = 0.30$. The premium charged to low risk customers is $P_L^* = \hat{P}_L = 0.217$. This yields expected profits for the low risk group of two, the cross-hatched area in Figure 5.3, that is, $[(0.217 - 0.100)(17.15)]$. Aggregate expected profits are only one since only half of the individuals are in the low risk class (that is, $N_L = 0.5$).

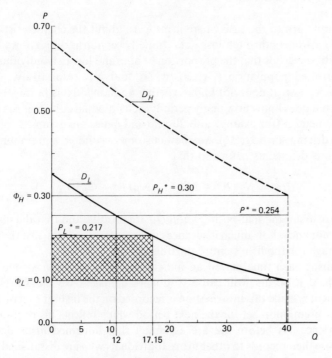

FIGURE 5.3 *Optimal premium structure by informed firms with perfect information*

Welfare Effects

In the no-information case, the equilibrium premium is P^* for both high and low risks. The availability of perfect information makes the low risks slightly better off, as the premium they pay falls to P^* or P_L, whichever is lower. If $P_L = P^*$, all of the gain from information goes to informed insurance firms in the form of higher profits. If $P_L = \hat{P}_L$, the low risk individual benefits by the amount that the monopoly profit maximizing price is below P^*. The higher risk consumers are made unequivocally worse off, since the premium they pay increases from P^* to Φ_H. Moreover, the positive profits being earned by informed firms are not eroded by entry, since new firms are by definition uninformed ones.

INFORMED FIRMS: LEARNING OVER TIME

Nature of Equilibrium

We now turn to the case where firms learn about the characteristics of their customers through loss data. Initially each firm only knows from statistical records that the proportion of high and low risk individuals in the insured population is given by N_H and N_L, respectively, where $N_H + N_L = 1$. It does not know whether an individual is in the H or L class but does know how many periods each potential customer has been in the market (for example, all 20-year-old males are assumed to have been driving since age 16). Any new customer is offered a premium, P^*, which is defined as before so that

$$E(\pi) = N_L(P^* - \Phi_L)Q_L + N_H(P^* - \Phi_H)Q_H = 0 \qquad (5.6)$$

We are assuming that both Q_L and Q_H are positive and that the insurer does not know how much insurance each person purchases, just the total coverage for the firm's entire portfolio.

During each time period an individual can suffer *at most* one loss, which, if it occurs, will cause X dollars damage. Any time a claims payment is made this information is recorded on the insurer's record and a new premium is set for the next period which reflects his overall loss experience. As before, we are assuming that informed firms do not disclose their records to other firms. Individuals who are dissatisfied with their new premium can seek insurance elsewhere. Other firms will not have access to the insured's record and hence cannot verify whether an applicant has had few or many losses under previous insurance contracts. Hence, uninformed firms just treat the individual as a new customer.

The informed firm uses a Bayesian updating process in readjusting its premium structure on the basis of its loss experience. All customers are assumed to have been with the same insurance company for exactly t periods, so they can have anywhere from 0 to t losses during this interval. The premium charged to individuals with j losses during a t period interval is $P_{jt}^*, j = 0, \ldots, t$.[7] Firms with loss experience data will set each premium P_{jt}^*, so that they maximize profits in period $t + 1$. Let w_{00}^L and w_{00}^H be the probabilities that an individual is in the low and high risk class when the firm initially insures him. We can update the probabilities by using Bayes' procedure. If a customer has suffered exactly j losses in a t period interval then we define $w_{jt}^i, i = L, H$ as the probability that he is in the ith risk class,[8] where $w_{jt}^H + w_{jt}^L = 1$. Naturally, the values of w_{jt}^i, $i = L, H$ depend on N_H and N_L as well as Φ_H and Φ_L. The premium set for each loss classification will also be determined in part by the relative values of $w_{jt}^i, i = L, H$. As j increases so does the probability that the individual is in the high risk class. Hence, $w_{jt}^H > w_{j-1,t}^H, j = 1, \ldots, t$.

The informed firm's process of determining an optimal set of premiums $\{P_{jt}^*\}$ is identical to the perfect information case detailed in the previous section. For each value of $P_{jt}, j = 1, \ldots, t$, one first determines the set of premiums charged by uninformed firms $\{P_{jt}''\}$ which yield zero expected profits in period $t + 1$. (Uninformed firms do not have the foresight to anticipate that current expected losses might be offset with future expected profits.)[9] The informed firms want to charge a set of premiums $\{P_{jt}^*\}$ in period $t + 1$ which guarantees that they will *not* lose any of their customers. The informed firms know that if an uninformed firm charges a premium $\{P_{jt}''\}$ it will attract all of their customers who pay more than this amount to the informed firm.

Suppose an informed firm offers a set of premiums $\{P_{jt}'\}$ with P_{jt}' increasing as j increases.[10] An uninformed firm who charged a lower premium than P_{jt}' would attract all customers with j or more losses.[11] The proportion of high and low customers in their portfolio is given by

$$W_{jt}^i = \left(\sum_{k=1}^{t} w_{kt}^i s_{kt} \right) \Big/ \sum_{k=j}^{t} s_{kt}$$

where s_{kt} = probability of a person suffering exactly k losses in a t period interval. In other words, W_{jt}^i is a weighted average over the loss range $j, \ldots, t$. Since w_{jt}^H increases with j we know that $W_{jt}^H > w_{jt}^H$ for all $j = 1, \ldots, t - 1$ and $W_{tt}^H = w_{tt}^H$.

The minimum premium (P''_{jt}) at which expected profit equals zero for uninformed firms is given by

$$W^H_{jt}(P''_{jt} - \Phi_H)Q^H_{jt} + W^L_{jt}(P''_{jt} - \Phi_L)Q^H_{jt} = 0 \qquad (5.7)$$

where Q^i_{jt} is demand for group i given a premium P''_{jt}. We know that P''_{jt} increases with j since W^H_{jt} increases with j. Hence any new firm who sets $P = P''_{jt}$ attracts only customers with j or more losses and makes zero expected profits. So equation (5.7) correctly describes the minimum level of premiums that uninformed firms can charge.

If the informed firms set $P_{jt} = P''_{jt} - \varepsilon$ for *only* those customers who have suffered exactly j losses, then these individuals will still prefer the informed firm. If the informed firm charges this premium, P_{jt}, to customers with j losses, its expected profits in period $t + 1$ are given by

$$w^H_{jt}(P_{jt} - \Phi_H)Q_H + w^L_{jt}(P_{jt} - \Phi_L)Q_L \geq 0 \qquad (5.8)$$

If $P_{jt} = P''_{jt} - \varepsilon$, then for sufficiently small ε, expected profits are positive for $j = 1, \ldots, t - 1$ since w^H_{jt} is less than W^H_{jt}. For $j = t$, as $\varepsilon \to 0$, profits by definition will also approach zero since $w^i_{tt} = W^i_{tt}$.

The premium structure for informed firms is now determined by finding the values $\{\hat{P}_{jt}\}$ for each $j = 0, \ldots, t$, which maximizes $E(\Pi_{jt})$, given by equation (5.8). It will keep all its customers and maximize expected profits for each loss category, if it sets premiums (P^*_{jt}) as follows

$$P^*_{jt} = \min \{P_{jt} - \varepsilon, \hat{P}_{jt}\}, j = 0, \ldots, t$$

The structure of the premiums is thus identical to the case of perfect information outlined above except that profits will be lower because firms must now use claims information to categorize their customers and, hence, will misclassify some of them. Aggregate expected profits for each period t are given by

$$E(\Pi_t) = \sum_{j=0}^{t} s_{jt} E(\Pi_{jt}) \qquad (5.9)$$

An Illustrative Example

An example using the same parameters as in the previous problem illustrates the differences between learning from loss experience and having perfect information on insured individuals. We will first determine the premium structure for customers who have been with the firm for one period and then show how the rates change as a customer's tenure with the firm increases.

Assume that $N_H = N_L = 0.5$, so that initially the firm sets the same premium as before – that is, $P^* = 0.254$ from equation (5.6). Table 5.1 illustrates how one calculates the weights for determining the optimal premium structure at the end of period 1 when $j = 0$ or 1, and Figure 5.4 details the optimal rate structure at the end of period 1. The optimal premiums are $P_{01}^* = 0.254$ and $P_{11}^* = 0.288$ since $\hat{P}_{01} = \hat{P}_{11} = 0.5$. The premium charged to the group suffering one loss (P_{11}^*), yields $E(\Pi_{11})= 0$ since $P_{11}^* = P_{11}''$, and $w_{11}^H = W_{11}^H$. Expected profits for the 'zero loss' class is given by equation (5.8) and is $E(\Pi_{01}) = 0.5625$ $(0.254 - 0.10)\,12 + 0.4375\,(0.254 - 0.30)\,40 = 0.23$. Aggregate expected profits for period 1 are given by equation (5.9) and in this case are $E(\Pi_1) = 0.8\,(0.23) = 0.18$.

It is worthwhile to focus on the welfare effects of experience rating when $t = 1$. In the case of two groups, those with the highest risk will either pay an actuarially fair rate or be subsidized by the low risk group. The misclassification of individuals thus always benefits those in the H class; either they are misclassified by being placed in the lower premium category (because they do not suffer a loss in period 1) or they suffer a loss but have a premium lower than Φ_H because some low risk individuals also have the bad luck to incur a loss in period 1. It also follows that the low risk individuals are charged premiums above Φ_L,

TABLE 5.1. *Calculation of weights* u_{jl}^i *and* $W_{jl}^i, i = L, H$ *for two period model* ($\Phi_L = 0.1; \Phi_H = 0.3; X = 40; c = 0.04; N_H = N_L = 0.5$)

j	s_{jl}	w_{jl}^H	w_{jl}^L	W_{jl}^H	W_{jl}^L
0	0.8	0.4375	0.5625	0.5	0.5
1	0.2	0.75	0.25	0.75	0.25

$$s_{01} = (1 - \Phi_H)(N_H) + (1 - \Phi_L)N_L$$

$$s_{11} = (\Phi_H)(N_H) + \Phi_L N_L$$

$$i = L, H \begin{cases} w_{01}^i = \{(1 - \Phi_i)N_i\}/s_{01} \\ w_{11}^i = (\Phi_i N_i)/s_{11} \\ W_{00}^i = \left(\sum_{k=0}^{1} w_{k1}^i s_{k1} \right) \Big/ \sum_{k=0}^{1} s_{k1} \\ W_{11}^i = w_{11}^i \end{cases}$$

TABLE 5.2 *Changes in premiums (P_jt), probabilities (S_jt), and expected profits [E(Π_jt)] for different times periods (t)*

Number of losses j		t = 0	1	2	3	4	5	10	15	20	25	30
0	$P_{0t} \rightarrow$	0.254	0.254	0.254	0.254	2.254	0.254	0.231	0.221	0.218	0.217	0.217
	$S_{0t} \rightarrow$	1	0.80	0.65	0.54	0.45	0.38	0.19	0.11	0.06	0.04	0.02
	$E(\Pi_{0t}) \rightarrow$	0	0.23	0.46	0.67	0.86	1.03	1.63	1.89	1.97	2.00	2.00
1	$P_{1t} \rightarrow$		0.288	0.286	0.285	0.283	0.281	0.272	0.232	0.221	0.218	0.217
	$S_{1t} \rightarrow$		0.20	0.30	0.34	0.35	0.34	0.25	0.19	0.14	0.10	0.07
	$E(\Pi_{1t}) \rightarrow$		0	0.06	0.13	0.23	0.34	1.00	1.60	1.88	1.97	2.00
2	$P_{2t} \rightarrow$			0.296	0.296	0.295	0.294	0.289	0.280	0.237	0.221	0.218
	$S_{2t} \rightarrow$			0.05	0.11	0.16	0.19	0.21	0.18	0.16	0.14	0.11
	$E(\Pi_{2t}) \rightarrow$			0	0.01	0.04	0.07	0.40	0.96	1.56	1.86	1.96
3	$P_3 \rightarrow$				0.299	0.299	0.298	0.296	0.293	0.287	0.235	0.222
	$S_{3t} \rightarrow$				0.01	0.04	0.07	0.16	0.15	0.13	0.13	0.12
	$E(\Pi_{3t}) \rightarrow$				0	0.004	0.01	0.11	0.43	0.92	1.53	1.85
4	$P_{4t} \rightarrow$					0.30	0.30	0.299	0.297	0.295	0.291	0.237
	$S_{4t} \rightarrow$					0.004	0.01	0.11	0.13	0.11	0.10	0.10
	$E(\Pi_{4t}) \rightarrow$					0	0.001	0.02	0.09	0.43	0.89	1.49
5	$P_{5t} \rightarrow$						0.30	0.30	0.299	0.298	0.296	0.294
	$S_{5t} \rightarrow$						0.001	0.05	0.11	0.11	0.08	0.07
	$E(\Pi_{5t}) \rightarrow$						0	0.004	0.03	0.13	0.42	0.85

	0	0.18	0.31	0.41	0.471	0.52	0.67	0.75	0.81	0.85	0.88
10						$P_{10t}\rightarrow$ $S_{10t}\rightarrow$ $E(\Pi_{10t})\rightarrow$	0.30 0.000+ 0	0.30 0.001 0	0.30 0.01 0	0.30 0.03 0	0.30 0.07 0
15							$P_{15t}\rightarrow$ $S_{15t}\rightarrow$ $E(\Pi_{15t})\rightarrow$	0.30 0.000+ 0	0.30 0.000+ 0	0.30 0.001 0	0.30 0.005 0
20								$P_{20t}\rightarrow$ $S_{20t}\rightarrow$ $E(\Pi_{20t})\rightarrow$	0.30 0.000+ 0	0.30 0.000+ 0	0.30 0.000+ $\mid 0$
25									$P_{25t}\rightarrow$ $S_{25t}\rightarrow$ $E(\Pi_{25t})\rightarrow$	0.30 0.000+ 0	0.30 0.000+ 0
30										$P_{30t}\rightarrow$ $S_{30t}\rightarrow$ $E(\Pi_{30t})\rightarrow$	0.30 0.000+ 0
$E(\Pi_t)\rightarrow$											

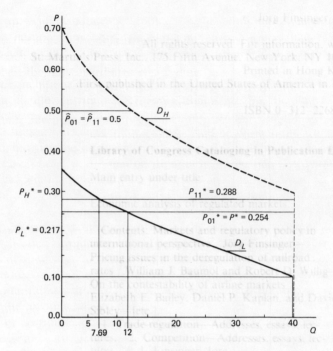

FIGURE 5.4 *Equilibrium premiums for two period example*

because of the firm's ability to exploit inside information. In the above example we see that the premium for low risk individuals would have been $P_L^* = 0.217$ if the firm had perfect information on each individual; it was actually $P_{11}^* = 0.288$ or $P_{01}^* = 0.254$ depending on whether or not the individual experienced a loss in period 1.

As a customer's life with the company increases then he faces a larger number of rate classes reflecting the possible outcomes. Table 5.2 details the scenario as t ranges from 0 to 30. This analysis clearly shows that firms make the largest profit on those customers who experience the fewest losses. Thus in Table 5.2 we see that expected profits for those individuals with zero losses $E(\Pi_{0t})$ increase from 0.23 to 2.00 as customers in this loss class decrease from $s_{01} = 0.8$ to $s_{0,30} = 0.02$.

Aggregate expected profits $E(\Pi_t)$ increase from 0.18 at the end of period 1 to 0.88 at the end of period 30. In the limit as $t \to \infty$, all customers will be accurately classified and we have the case of perfect information where aggregate expected profits are 1, as shown in the illustrative example at the end of the second section. Figure 5.5 graphically depicts how aggregate expected profit changes over time as a

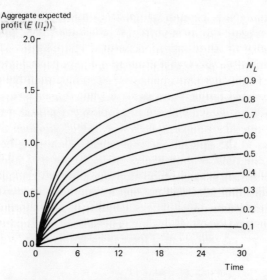

FIGURE 5.5   *Aggregate expected profits* $[E(\Pi_t)]$ *as a function of proportion of low risk customers* (N_L) *and time* (t).

function of proportion of low risk customers in the population. As N_L decreases then the informed firm's profit potential decreases since a larger proportion of individuals will suffer losses.

Interpretation of Learning Model

The single period equilibrium model has an interesting interpretation in the context of Cyert and March's (1963) study on the behavioral theory of the firm and Williamson's (1975) work on impacted information. Suppose we view policyholders as an integral part of the firm, as in a mutual insurance company where every insured individual is a member of the company. Any time there is a subsidy we can refer to this situation as one of organizational slack. As defined by Cyert and March, 'slack consists in payments to members of the coalition in excess of what is required to maintain the organization' (p. 36). This concept is mainly of interest because it implies greater stability of the firm. In the context of this example, slack applies to those in the highest risk class who have no economic incentive to leave their insurance firm because their premiums are either actuarially fair or being subsidized.

The low risk group has the reverse reaction – all the members are being charged more than the actuarial rate but other firms cannot distinguish their special status because of impacted information. They are thus forced to remain with their current firm because others in the industry are not privy to the information on their relative risk. At the risk of generalization, we find that if firms do not have perfect information on their clients, insured individuals who are worse than the average will remain because of organizational slack while those who are better than average will not switch because of problems of impacted informâtion.

Extensions of the Model

The model of firm behavior was based on a number of simplifying short-term equilibrium assumptions which can now be relaxed *without* changing the basic qualitative results regarding equilibrium: viz, entry will be restricted in an industry where firms have inside information and monopoly profits will result if there is no regulation.

Increasing the Number of Risk Classes

As the number of risk classes increases the computations become more complicated but the nature of the solution remains the same as in the above case. The highest risk class will either pay the actuarial rate or be subsidized by the lower risk classes. Firms will make profits by exploiting their inside knowledge that some individuals are good risks. Firms without these data cannot determine whether an applicant has had few or many losses; hence, they have to assume he is an average individual.

Imperfect Information by Consumers

If consumers do not have accurate estimates of the risks they are facing then firms can exploit this imperfection if they have statistical data on which to base their estimates. Even if they cannot identify the risk category of each individual they can charge a set of premiums which maximizes their profits subject to the constraint that no entering firm can capture their customers. We thus have a mixture of a purely competitive market and monopoly in determining the final rates. As R–S and others, have shown, a stable competitive market will lead to a premium based on the true risk even if consumers misperceive it. Otherwise a firm can enter and make positive profits by charging a premium slightly above the actuarial rate. In our model, imperfect information will have no impact on the rate-setting process for any values of $P_{jt}^* = P_{jt}''$. Whenever the firm finds that $P_{jt}^* = \hat{P}_{jt} < P_{jt}''$ it will then take advantage of inaccuracies by the consumer by setting a rate (P_{jt}^{**}) based on consumer misperceptions of the risk.[12]

CONCLUSIONS

Implications for Regulation

The single period equilibrium model appears to describe real world behavior because both the consumer and firm have imperfect information. More specifically, the empirical evidence on consumer decision processes regarding insurance purchase behavior suggests that most individuals have limited knowledge of premiums or available coverage (Kunreuther *et al.*, 1978). Hence we hypothesize that one would expect that few consumers attempt to obtain information on how their premiums will be adjusted with experience. They undoubtedly have a vague notion that such adjustments occur, but have no written information on their insurance policy as to what these changes are. Furthermore, an insurer cannot distinguish between new purchasers and bad risks seeking a better deal.

In this situation there are potential welfare gains from regulation. In particular, experience rating makes bad risks worse off, good risks only slightly better off, and it transfers most of the gains in the form of monopoly rents to insurers. These rents are not eroded by entry. Ideal regulation should not, however, mandate uniform (non-experience) or community rating. Instead, it should require that premiums be set close to the actuarial experience for each class of risks. This can either be done by requiring data on actuarial experience, or simply by regulating the rate of return. By forcing firms to disclose personal information on their customers, insured individuals will be better off since monopoly profits will be eroded away.

Future Empirical Research

The concept of experience rating over time suggests reasons for job classification schemes in much the same way that insurance systems have rate classification schemes. In this sense the models developed in this paper complement the important work of Spence (1973) on market signalling which provides a way of classifying individuals on the basis of observable traits such as educational status. There still may be difficulties in distinguishing between 'good' and 'bad' risks, but these information imperfections will be reduced to the extent that a particular variable is an accurate discriminator.

Another relevant question relates to the implications for market behavior if firms use, or are forced to use, updating procedures which differ from the Bayesian ones described above. For example, suppose firms have only three or four rate classifications no matter what happens to an individual and no matter how many periods he has been insured with a firm. In several European countries an individual who has had no losses for a certain number of consecutive years is automatically placed in the lowest rate classification. How would such regulatory constraints affect the equilibria for the high and low risk groups?

A final, and in many ways fundamental matter, is the development of a model of insurance premium setting. An individual or group's past experience is not the only information available to the insurance firm; premiums in practice depend both on experience and on certain individual characteristics, such as age, sex, marital status, and so on. How should all of this information be used in determining a particular individual's premium, either from the viewpoint of Pareto optimality or from the viewpoint of competitive survival? How might imperfectly informed consumers interact with imperfectly informed firms? These questions are beyond the scope of this chapter but suggest fruitful areas for increasing our understanding of insurance markets.

NOTES

1. The research report in this paper is supported by the Bundesministerium für Forschung und Technologie, FRG, contract no. 321/7591/RGB 8001. While support for this work is gratefully acknowledged, the views expressed are the authors' and not necessarily shared by the sponsor. We gratefully express our appreciation to Jörg Finsinger and Paul Kleindorfer for comments on an earlier draft of this paper, to participants in the Conference on Economics of Regulation in Berlin for their helpful suggestions, and to Serge Medow for his computational assistance.
2. One of the purposes of experience rating is to cope with problems of moral hazard. It does this by rewarding those who do not make claims on their policy in period t with lower premiums in the next period. This paper does not answer the question analytically as to whether this type of premium adjustment process eliminates or substantially reduces moral hazard, but it does show that the firm captures much of the differential information provided by data on claims.
3. Indeed, the signal is so good that, if all individuals have the same utility function, the mere decision to purchase a particular quantity of insurance signals the individual's risk class; a person who has signalled that he is low

risk by choosing the small quantity policy could then be offered full coverage at a rate near the actuarial level for good risks. Hence, even when R–S equilibrium occurs, it may be dominated by such a strategy. Of course, this new strategy may itself be dominated as consumers learn to respond by offering false signals about their initial most preferred policy.

4. When the only value of P which satisfies (2) is $P^* = \Phi_H$, then $Q_L = 0$, and the market fails.

5. If $\hat{P}_L$ is less than P^*, then the informed firm will always charge $P_H^I = \Phi_H$ and $P_L^I = \hat{P}_L$ making positive profits. Uninformed firms will not obtain any business no matter what they do.

6. A more detailed discussion of this model appears in Kunreuther (1976).

7. We are assuming that losses for an individual are independent of previous experience so the premium at the end of t is determined only by the number of claims.

8. We determine w_{jt} as follows.

Let V_{jt}^L = probability that an individual experiences j losses in t periods if he is risk class i.

Specifically

$$V_{jt}^L = \frac{t!}{(t-j)!\,j!}\,(\Phi_i)^j (1-\Phi_i)^{t-j}$$

using Bayes' formula

$$w_{jt}^L = (V_{jt}^L N_L)/\sum V_{jt}^L N_L$$

9. See Kunreuther and Pauly (1981) for a 'foresight' model.

10. We will show below that P_{jt}^* increases as j increases.

11. We are assuming no transaction costs for insured individuals to switch firms.

12. The informed firm will still be constrained to set $P_{jt}^{**} \leqslant P_{jt}''$ so that it may only be able to partially capitalize on consumer misperceptions.

REFERENCES

Cyert, R. and J. March (1963) *A Behavioral Theory of the Firm* (Englewood Cliffs, N.J. : Prentice-Hall).

Dahlby, B. (1980) 'Adverse Selection and Pareto Improvements Through Compulsory Insurance', (mimeo).

Follman, Joseph, Jr. (1963) *Medical Care and Health Insurance* (Homewood, Ill.: Irwin) ch. 18.

Grossman, H. (1979) 'Adverse Selection, Dissembling and Competitive Equilibrium', *Bell Journal of Economics*, 10, 336–43.

Jaynes, G. (1978) 'Equilibria in Monopolistically Competitive Insurance Markets', *Journal of Economic Theory*, 19, 394–422.

Johnson, W. (1978) 'Overinsurance and Public Provision of Insurance: Comment', *Quarterly Journal of Economics*, 92, 693–6.

Kunreuther, H. (1976) 'Limited Knowledge and Insurance Protection', *Public Policy*, 24, 227–61.

Insurance Markets

Kunreuther, H. and M. Pauly (1981) 'Market Equilibrium with Learning: Experience Rating of Insurance', mimeo.

Kunreuther, H. *et al.* (1978) *Disaster Insurance Protection* (New York: Wiley).

Miyasaki, H. (1977) 'The Rat Race and Internal Labor Markets', *The Bell Journal of Economics*, 8, 394–418.

Pauly, M. (1974) 'Over Insurance and Public Provision of Insurance: The Roles of Moral Hazard and Adverse Selection', *Quarterly Journal of Economics*, 88, 44–62.

Rothschild, M. and J. Stiglitz (1976) 'Equilibrium in Competitive Insurance Markets: An Essay in the Economics of Imperfect Information', *Quarterly Journal of Economics*, 90, 629–49.

Spence, M. (1973) 'Job Market Signaling', *Quarterly Journal of Economics*, 87, 355–74.

Spence, M. (1978) 'Product Differentiation and Consumer Choice in Insurance Markets', *Journal of Public Economics*, 10, 427–47.

Williamson, O. (1975) *Markets and Hierarchies* (New York: The Free Press).

Wilson, C. (1977) 'A Model of Insurance Markets with Incomplete Information', *Journal of Economic Theory*, 16, 167–207.

6 Competition, Ownership and Control in Markets with Imperfect Information[1]

JÖRG FINSINGER

THE GERMAN INSURANCE INDUSTRY

The private insurance industry is the fastest growing branch of the German industry. Its relative share in gross value added has doubled in the period between 1960 and 1976. In 1977, the average household spent 2358 DM on insurance, adding up to 4.7 per cent of GNP.

It is generally held that competition in this market allocates resources efficiently and that market performance is acceptable. Also, it is generally accepted that the regulatory agency serves an important role in making competition viable, where many real and imaginary market failures may hurt consumers. We present some institutional details, some simple theory of firm behavior and, finally, some casual evidence, and we conclude that certain regulatory policies create market intransparency and, thereby, cause market failure.

INSTITUTIONAL CONSTRAINTS ON COMPETITION IN GERMAN LIABILITY AND LIFE INSURANCE MARKETS

Since 1901, when the Law for Insurance Regulation was passed, the most prominent argument for regulation has been consumer protection. 'The social and ethical role of insurance has to be protected, because even the diligent and careful consumer is unable to evaluate insurance

111

institutions'.[2] This is why a regulatory agency was established and given control over all competitive parameters of the industry.

Entry

Insurance companies must first obtain a licence by submitting a proposal for the planned business operations. Minimum capital requirements have to be met, the proposed premiums have to guarantee the firm's long run viability, the proposed insurance contract conditions have to conform to regulatory standards, and careful estimates of administrative costs, marketing costs and of the required reinsurance have to be given. This plan of business operations has to be updated at regular intervals. The agency has the necessary rights to enforce compliance with the plan.

In order to prevent cross-subsidization each firm can only be licensed for certain lines of insurance. Licences for life, liability, health, credit and legal suit insurance are deemed to be incompatible.

Premiums

In general, premium calculation must reflect all costs such that the long run viability of the firm is insured. Within the boundaries given by this precaution the firms can set premiums freely. More stringent standards apply to the main lines of insurance – automobile, life and health insurance – where premiums must be approved by the agency. There the level of premiums is determined by rate of return on premiums or capital considerations.

Profit Regulation

Automobile Insurance

Automobile insurance tariffs are determined as the sum of the risk premium, administrative costs and commissions to agents and a safety margin, plus a 3 per cent rate of return on total premiums written. The risk premium is taken to be the same for all firms and is equal to the average industry loss experience unless a firm can prove it has had a lower loss experience for at least five consecutive years or shows a significantly higher loss experience. Projected administrative costs are based on the previous year's experience. Commissions cannot exceed 11 per cent of premiums. *Ex ante*, a profit margin of 3 per cent return on total premiums written is conceded. Thus, premium regulation establishes a conservative lower bound on automobile insurance tariffs. Insolvency is effectively prevented, but *ex post* profits may be large.[3]

This is why *ex post* profit regulation requires firms to return excess profits to the insured. The exact rate of return regulations are given in Table 6.1.

TABLE 6.1   *Ex post profit regulation*

Surplus in percentage of premiums	Allowed surplus share	Minimum ex post rebate
up to 3	1	0
3–6	0	1
6–15	1/3	2/3
above 15	0	1

Take for instance a company whose pretax surplus amounts to 12 per cent of premiums. It can retain 3 per cent + 1/3 (12 per cent − 6 per cent) = 5 per cent and has to return 1 (6 per cent − 3 per cent) + 2/3 (12 per cent − 6 per cent) = 7 per cent to its customers.

Life Insurance

Government promotes life-insurance by exempting the returns to the insured or the beneficiaries from taxation. Also, depending on income, the premiums can be fully or partly deducted from the income tax paid. This is why most life insurance contracts are composed of a risk and a savings component. The contract stipulates the amount of money a policy holder or the beneficiary is entitled to:

in case of death,
at the end of the contract period.

The mean length of currently written contracts is 28 years. Irrespective of the rate of return on the invested capital or of the interest rate, premiums are required to be fixed for the whole contract length. They must be calculated according to the death statistics of 1960/1962 plus a safety margin. In those days life expectancy was significantly lower than today. The projected (nominal) rate of return is taken to be 3 per cent when the average (nominal) return is about 7 per cent. Thus, the risk and the savings premiums are higher than necessary. In particular, these two components of the total premium as well as the administrative cost

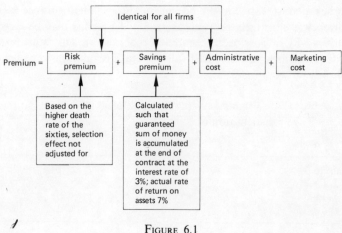

FIGURE 6.1

component are the same for all firms irrespective of their individual performance.

The only firm specific premium component is the marketing cost. The agency has always attempted, in particular, to contain the substantial marketing cost share by setting a low upper bound on these costs. With very few exceptions the bound is exceeded and thus must be used as the basis for the premium calculation procedure. As a consequence, premiums are almost identical for all companies. Note how the attempt of the agency to contain marketing costs eliminates price competition, thereby shifting the competitive effort to marketing and ultimately increasing marketing costs.

Given these conditions it is not surprising that the average surplus in the German life insurance industry amounted to 33 per cent of premiums in 1978. The regulatory agency therefore requires the life insurance companies to return at least 90 per cent of this surplus to the insured. In fact, all insurance companies return more than this minimum. However, only very few companies return the surplus immediately to the insured. Most of them keep the surplus in special accounts until the end of the contract and make further handsome profits on their customers' capital.

Uniformity of Contracts

As stated by regulatory law the main objective of insurance regulation is the protection of consumers. In the eyes of the regulators the most prominent means to this end is a restriction on the variety of contracts.

Contract clauses must be standardized within each line of insurance. This aim has been attained in automobile insurance, where all companies offer identical contracts for all risk classes. The risk classes are specified by the agency in terms of certain objective characteristics of the car and its owner. However, such contract uniformity could not be achieved in the life insurance industry, due ultimately to the elimination of price competition. Virtually all life insurance companies have chosen different schemes for the distribution of the regulation-induced surpluses. There are numerous schemes for apportioning the surpluses to the individual contracts, either to the risk component (paid out in case of death) or to the savings component (paid out at the end of the contract). In this line of insurance price uniformity was obtained at the cost of complete lack of transparency for the distribution of excess surplus. Even many life insurance salesmen do not seem to know or understand their companies' complicated schemes.

The regulatory impact of interest in the context of this chapter is easily summarized:

In the automobile insurance market contracts are uniform, but net premiums, *ex ante* premium minus *ex post* rebate, are uncertain.

In the life insurance market premiums are almost uniform, but contracts are highly differentiated. Complicated profit sharing schemes combined with the large discretionary powers of the firm managers cloud the real value of contracts.

PROPERTY RIGHTS AND MARKET BEHAVIOUR

The debate on ownership and control is ultimately a debate on management behaviour. Does management maximize profits, sales or managerial utility or does it satisfice – that is, does it satisfy minimal levels with respect to several objectives? To answer this question the relationship between management compensation and firm variables has been investigated. It can be shown that management compensation increases with firm size, but after allowing for this effect, management compensation is positively associated with profits.[4] There is also the Marris and Manne theory, that managerial discretion is limited by takeover bids. Finally, we have the Darwinian argument that profit maximization is forced upon firms by the competitive process, and that management slack leads to bankruptcy.

This latter argument does not hold for insurance markets. Bankruptcy is prevented by regulation. Also, regulation reduces price competition by making real prices uncertain. Therefore competitive pressure may be weaker than in other markets and consequently discretionary management behaviour is more likely.[5] In particular, we expect to see systematic differences of management decisions between firms of different ownership structure.

Three different types of firms supply insurance: stock companies, mutual companies and public enterprises. The profit motive is plausible only for the management of stock companies. Mutual companies do not make profits by their very constitution; all surplus is ultimately returned to the insured. The same is true for public enterprises.[6] Nonetheless, neither of the two firm types are run by the insured. In fact the management is only initially elected by the insured and is then replaced by cooption. In this respect mutual companies differ from public enterprises only when they are constituted. The insured only meet once as members to elect the first group of managers; thereafter, the management is on its own.

Historically, the members of mutual companies wielded some power. However, as the companies grew the members became less involved in the decision processes and now even their liability to pay for company losses has been shifted to reinsurance companies. In this sense the status of the members has become identical to the status of the stock company clients. This fact leads to the widely held view that there are no systematic management related differences between firms of different ownership structure.[7] Later on, the fallacy of this argument will be shown.

Before turning to empirical evidence for regulation-induced market failure simple models of management decisions will be presented. The decisions of a rate-of-return-regulated profit-motivated management are compared to the decisions of a sales-maximizing management.

PRICE AND QUALITY DECISIONS UNDER DIFFERENT MANAGEMENT OBJECTIVES IN AUTOMOBILE INSURANCE MARKETS

Regulated Profit Maximizing Behavior

The Price and Quality Choice

As explained in the second section, the profits from automobile insurance are restricted to a fair rate of return on premiums. The impact of such a regulatory constraint will now be analyzed in a simple theoretical model. Consider a firm offering automobile insurance at price p and quality q. Let $x(p, q)$ denote the demand or sales function. Since consumers do not have complete information, the firm has a certain amount of market power. Thus, for given q_0, $x(p, q_0)$ is downward sloping or, in terms of the inverse demand function, $p(x, q)$, we have $\dfrac{\partial p}{\partial x} < 0$.

The cost of producing x insurance policies of quality q is given by cxq, $c > 0$. Constant returns to scale with respect to output may be justified for liability insurance by the findings of P. Joskow (1973). Constant returns with respect to the quality index q is less restrictive than it seems, for the quality index is defined up to an arbitrary monotonic transformation.

The profit of the firm can now be written as

$$\pi = px - cqx$$

Since profit π is restricted to a fair return on premiums

$$\pi \leq \alpha px; \quad 0 < \alpha < 1$$

If this constraint is binding the following optimality conditions can be derived, the subscript p denoting the profit maximizing firm's decision variables:

P1 $p_p = (cq_p)/(1 - \alpha)$

P2 $\partial p_p / \partial q = [c\{1 - (1/e_p)\}]/(1 - \alpha)$

where

$$e_p = -(\partial x_p / \partial p)\,(p_p / x_p)$$

is the price elasticity of demand. The price rule $P1$ means an increase of price p_p above marginal cost cq_p by the factor $1/(1 - \alpha) > 1$. The quality choice rule $P2$ will be analyzed in the following section.

The Rate of Return and the Quality Choice

The fair rate of return on premiums α is set by the regulatory agency. Therefore, it should be of interest that in general the quality of service q_p declines as α is increased. Substituting $t = 1/(1 - \alpha)$ into $P1$ and $P2$ and completing the comparative statics

$$dq/dt = c(\Gamma/\Delta)$$

where

$$\Gamma = \left(x \frac{\partial^2 p}{\partial x^2} + 2 \frac{\partial p}{\partial x} - \frac{\partial^2 p}{\partial x \partial q} q \right)$$

$$\Delta = \frac{\partial p}{\partial x} \left\{ \frac{\partial^2 p}{\partial q^2} - tc \frac{x}{p} \left(\frac{\partial^2 p}{\partial x \partial q} - \frac{\partial p}{\partial x} \frac{\partial p}{\partial q} \frac{1}{p} \right) \right\}$$
$$+ \frac{\partial p}{\partial x} \frac{x}{p} \left\{ \frac{tc}{p} \left(x \frac{\partial^2 p}{\partial x^2} + \left(1 + \frac{1}{e} \right) \frac{\partial p}{\partial x} \right) - \frac{\partial^2 p}{\partial x \partial q} \right\}$$

Note that $\partial p/\partial x$ in general increases with q, that is, $\partial^2 p/(\partial x \partial q) \geq 0$.

Consider $\{\partial x(p, q)\}/\partial p$ at a given price level p. At a low quality level q_L a slight price decrease $\Delta p < 0$ leads to a smaller sales increase Δx_L than at a higher quality level q_H, $\Delta x_H > \Delta x_L > 0$.[8] Hence, we expect

$$(\partial x/\partial p)(p, q_H) < (\partial x/\partial p)(p, q_L)$$

or

$$\partial^2 p/(\partial x \partial q) \geq 0$$

provided $\partial p^2/\partial x^2 \leq 0$; but then $\Gamma \leq 0$ and $\Delta \geq 0$ follow. Hence, we have $\partial q/\partial t < 0$ or quality decreases as α increases.

Variable Cost Distortion

Before comparing $P1$ and $P2$ to the decision rules under other forms of management objectives, reconsider the assumption of minimum cost production. We now show that the regulatory constraint may well raise variable cost above the minimum cost level. Suppose for any given amount of (security) capital K the minimum variable cost of producing output x of quality q is given by $v(q, x, K)$. Also, assume decreasing marginal variable cost savings with increasing capital intensity, that is, $v_{KK} > 0$ and obviously $v_K < 0$. Thus we allow short run marginal cost to deviate from long run marginal cost; for equality we must have

$$(\partial v/\partial K) + r = 0$$

Under these assumptions the regulatory constraint can be written as

$$px - v \leq \alpha px$$

For the regulatory agency measures profit or rather surplus as revenues minus variable cost. The allowed costs do not include a fair return on capital. It can now easily be shown that the regulated profit-maximizing firm does not choose cost-minimizing factor inputs. It produces at higher variable costs than is efficient. It chooses K, x and q such that

$$(\partial v/\partial K) + r = \lambda(\partial v/\partial K) < 0$$

where $\lambda > 0$ is the Lagrangian multiplier corresponding to the rate of return constraint.

But another theoretical argument for inflated variable costs can be given. Consumer search for low priced offers is discouraged by uncertainty about the yearly rebate. *Ex ante* price may be high, but the rebate may be high or low. Also, the eligibility for rebates varies from company to company and from year to year. In general, drivers with low loss experience ratings are favoured. But this knowledge is hardly sufficient as a guide for price comparisons. Consequently, buyers are insensitive to small price differences at least. Hence, in the neighbourhood of the mean price and most certainly below the mean price, the price elasticity of demand may be below 1 for a given level of quality. Now, $P1$ and $P2$ imply that the monopolist will not set prices in this range. He will increase price until the elasticity equals or exceeds 1. This price increase raises revenues without additional cost. Profits go up and may exceed the allowed return on revenues px

$$px - c \leq \alpha px$$

There is only one way to avoid excess returns; the inflation of cost. Cost can be inflated by marketing efforts and by investing in quality, or simply by inefficient production. Also, there is an incentive to deceive the regulators by manipulating cost figures in the balance sheets. This incentive is most serious when the returns to marketing and quality increases are low.

The Sales Maximizing Firm

A sales maximizing firm must solve the following problem:

$$\max_{x,\, q} \quad p(x, q)x$$

such that $p(x, q)x - cqx \geq 0$

Note that the regulatory constraint is not binding. There is only the viability constraint that revenues exceed cost. The decision rules corresponding to $P1$ and $P2$ are

S1 $\quad p_s = cq_s$

S2 $\quad p_s/\partial q = c\{1 - (1/e_s)\}$

Recalling the comparative statics result in the section concerned with the rate of return and the quality choice, $P1$ and $P2$ are transformed into $S1$ and $S2$ as $t = 1/(1 - \alpha)$ approaches 1 or as α approaches 0. We conclude that the sales maximizing firm chooses higher quality than the profit maximizer. Also, we see that the current rate of return regulation modifies profit maximizing behaviour towards sales maximizing behaviour.

Summary

We compared price and quality decision rules for the profit and the sales maximizing firm. Our findings are summarized in Table 6.2. They also hold for a Cournot–Nash type of market equilibrium with many firms when each firm faces the same demand function $x(p, q)$, that is, when consumers only form expectations about price and quality variables and when their decision is not influenced by any other considerations.

TABLE 6.2

Choice	Objective	
	Sales	Profits
Price rule	$p_s = cq_s$	$p_p = (cq_p)/(1 - \alpha)$
Product quality		$q_s > q_p$

In the section concerned with variable cost distortion it was shown that the currently used form of rate of return regulation induces the profit motivated monopolist to produce at inflated cost. In a section below we present empirical evidence for this induced inefficiency.

In the section concerned with the rate of return and the quality choice it was shown that the quality of service of the rate of return regulated monopolist declines as the rate of return is increased.

SOME EMPIRICAL EVIDENCE FROM THE AUTOMOBILE INSURANCE MARKET

Ownership, Marketing and the Price–Quality Relationship

Data was collected on 72 insurance companies constituting 91.2 per cent of the market. Only the smallest firms were excluded from the sample. Most companies use exclusive agents for the sales of contracts. Some stock companies and the majority of the mutual companies use direct marketing; they sell insurance mostly in exclusive bureaux. Thus, five categories of firms can be distinguished (see Table 6.3).

TABLE 6.3   *Market share and number of firms*

	Stock Companies	Mutual Companies	Public Enterprises	Total
Exclusive	69.0%	5.4%	4.6%	79.0%
agents	48	6	5	59
Direct	1.1%	11.1%	0%	12.2%
marketing	6	7	0	13
	70.1%	16.5%	4.6%	91.2%
All firms	54	13	5	72

The regulatory agency supplied the number of complaints about individual firms by dissatisfied customers for the first six months of 1980. For each firm this number was divided by the market share and taken as an index of the quality of service.[9] An analysis of variance revealed that ownership structure has an effect on this quality index (significant at the 5% level). The deviations from the mean are given in Table 6.4.

Similarly, premium levels were related to firm type as well as to marketing policy. Ownership structure as well as the marketing policy have a significant impact (at the 1% level) on premium level. The cell means deviations are given in Table 6.4. Also, the deviations of premiums adjusted for the mean rebate of stock and mutual companies as well as of public enterprises were calculated.

Table 6.4 suggests that consumers should prefer mutual companies to stock companies. For both types of marketing policy mutual companies show a superior price–quality relationship. But then, how is it that stock companies survive in the market? The answer is obvious. First, consumers do not sufficiently learn the differences in service quality. Second, the regulated *ex ante* premiums differ less than the *ex post*

TABLE 6.4 *Index of complaints and premium levels (percentage deviations from the mean)*

		Stock Companies	Mutual Companies	Public Enterprises
Exclusive agents	Index of complaints	+1%	−2%	−54%
	Premium levels (*ex ante*)	+1%	−1%	−2%
	Premium levels (adjusted for rebates)	±0%	−3%	−9%
Direct marketing	Index of complaints	+63%	−27%	
	Premium levels (*ex ante*)	−4%	−4%	
	Premium levels (adjusted for rebates)	−7%	−13%	

premiums adjusted for rebates. Consumers cannot form realistic expectations about future rebates.

Public enterprises seem to provide higher quality of service at lower premiums than mutual companies or stock companies. A comparison of Tables 6.4 and 6.2 suggests that stock company performance could be explained by the impact of the regulatory constraint on profit maximizing behaviour. However, it should be noted that the analysis of variance results only prove that ownership structure has a significant impact on premium level and on the quality index. The analysis of variance does not provide a rigorous test for the models developed in the section concerned with price and quality decisions under different management objectives. In fact, such a test was never intended. For it seems obvious that the pure management strategies, profit, sales or welfare maximization will not adequately describe actual firm behaviour. Observable firm behaviour will rather be a 'mix' of these ideal types.

Regulation Induced Inefficiency

Even though observable firm behavior may not be 'idealtypisch' in the Weberian sense, it is clear that the regulatory rate of return constraint can only be binding for stock companies. For all other companies profits are excluded by their very constitution. As shown in the section concerned with variable cost distortion, the rate of return constraint may lead to inflated costs. This is why we calculated the administrative costs as well as the marketing costs (commissions) as a fraction of premiums.

TABLE 6.5   *Cost as percentage of premiums*

Year	1970	1975	1977
Stock Companies:			
Commissions	11.8	10.2	10.9
Administration	12.7	9.8	9.7
Mutual Companies:			
Commissions	6.8	5.6	5.9
Administration	8.4	7.6	7.1
Public Enterprises:			
Commissions	10.5	8.6	9.8
Administration	9.2	8.7	9.1

SOURCE   Veröffentlichungen des Bundesaufsichtsamtes für Versicherungswesen, vols 27, 1978, and 28, 1979.

Note that since the stock companies generally charge higher premiums their cost ratios are under-estimated in terms of real output.[10] Table 6.5 gives the cost ratios for the different types of firms.[11]

It is not surprising that the commission costs of stock companies by far exceed those of mutual companies, because these costs reflect the use of agents for marketing. However, it is surprising to find a 2.5 per cent difference in administrative costs between stock companies and mutual companies. This difference suggests that the rate of return constraint on stock companies either induces cost inefficiency or leads to a mis-representation of actual costs.

In addition to these marked cost differences, there is evidence for substitution of reinsurance for capital. Stock companies rely more heavily on reinsurance and show a lower visible capital/gross premiums ratio than public enterprises or mutual companies. This effect is consistent with the results in the section concerned with variable cost distortions.

TABLE 6.6   *Reinsurance activity and capital*

	Stock Companies	Mutual Companies	Public Enterprises
Fraction of gross premiums retained	61%	75%	87%
Visible capital as percentage of gross premiums	19%	20%	26%

SOME EMPIRICAL EVIDENCE OF MARKET FAILURE IN GERMAN LIFE INSURANCE MARKETS

Market Transparency and Performance Indicators

There is no price competition in the German life insurance market. Regulation imposes almost uniform premiums on all companies in spite of large differences in performance (see the section on institutional constraints on competition above). These differences may persist over long periods of time because consumers lack the relevant information. In fact, some of the accessible information is misleading. Only partial performance indicators are published, some of which play a central role in signalling firm performance to consumers. Companies make an effort to improve such partial indicators without improving overall performance thereby hurting customers' interests in the long run.

In 1975 the yearly report of the regulatory agency stated that some companies return much less surplus to the accounts of the insured than others. For the comparison a partial indicator of performance, the RE-Quota (Rückerstattungsquote) was used. The RE-Quota is basically the fraction of surplus put into the special accounts of the insured to be paid out at the end of the contract period. The RE-Quota is indeed a very partial indicator of performance. Even if the surplus is small due to inefficient operations the firm may still transfer a large fraction of surplus to the return accounts. In spite of this fact the RE-Quota became a widely used indicator. It was estimated[12] by business magazines such as *Capital* and the consumer magazine *Test*. Firms began to manipulate the RE-Quota, wasting resources rather than improving performance.

Another indicator, the UE-Quota, is still reported.[13] It gives the fraction of surplus which is retained in the company. A third indicator of performance, the current return on invested assets, is similarly misleading. It does not reflect realized capital gains such as the sale of property or other assets with low book value. Fortunately, the business magazine *Capital* has recently begun to report more relevant performance indicators reflecting cost efficiency, marketing expenses, early cancellation of contracts, and so on. Thus, consumers now have access to more complete information on performance variables. It is, however, doubtful whether they are able to interpret the multitude of indicators correctly. In particular, it is still impossible to rank firms according to overall performance. Nonetheless, this lack of market transparency seems less harmful than the misleading transparency of those days when only the RE-Quota was available. Firms now have less incentive to manipulate partial indicators of performance.

Performance Indicators and Firm Ownership

Data on the following performance indicators were collected from *Capital* as well as from the regulatory agency.

K79	total cost as percentage of total premium revenues for 1979;
BK75/79	operating cost as percentage of premium, total cost minus allowed marketing cost for 1975–9;
S79	number of early cancellations of contracts as percentage of total number of contracts in 1979;
GR79	rate of return on mean invested capital for 1979;
BEGM	number of complaints divided by market share, counting only complaints which were classified as justified by the regulatory agency;
UE79	UE-Quota, fraction of surplus retained in the company for 1979.

These performance indicators were related to the relevant firm characteristics. As firm dummies all those variables were included which are assumed to have an impact on operations.

OSHIP	ownership: public enterprise, stock company, mutual company;[14]
M	marketing: direct marketing, use of agents;
A	age of company: established if older than 10 years, young if younger than 10 years;
B	client specialization: customers only amongst civil servants (Beamte) and employees of state enterprises;
KMIX	client specialization: Kleinleben if firm sells a disproportionate amount of small 'Kleinleben' contracts which are considered to cause higher cost than other contracts, Normix otherwise

In Tables 6.7–6.17 we present the analysis of variance results.

TABLE 6.7   *Sample description*

	Stock Companies	Mutual Companies	Public Enterprises	Total
Market share	67.6%	23.4%	9%	100%
Number of firms	52	36	12	100
Average market share per firm	1.30%	0.65%	0.75%	

In this chapter we interpret only the results pertaining to ownership. Whenever ownership makes a significant difference, public enterprises out-perform mutual companies,[15] which in turn out-perform stock companies. Take for example total cost as a fraction of premium revenues: on the average 28.9 per cent of all premiums are eaten up by the cost of operation.[16] However, public enterprises only spend 21 per cent of premium revenues on administration and marketing as compared to 28.2 per cent for mutual companies and 31.2 per cent for stock companies. There is no significant difference between the respective returns on invested capital. Now, recall that public enterprises as well as mutual companies ultimately return all profits to the insured. Consequently, consumers do better when buying from these two firm types than from stock companies. The two reported quality indicators only strengthen this conclusion. The fraction of early cancellations, S79,

TABLE 6.8   *Analysis of variance (K79 by OSHIP M, A, B, KMIX)*

Source of variation	Sum of squares	DF	Mean square	F	Significance of F
Main effects	3705	6	617	15.0	0.001
OSHIP	488	2	244	5.9	0.004
M	470	1	470	11.4	0.001
A	1505	1	1505	36.6	0.001
B	65	1	65	1.5	0.211
KMIX	630	1	630	15.3	0.001
Two-way interactions	152	4	38	0.9	0.453
OSHIP A	44	1	44	1.0	0.302
OSHIP B	120	2	60	1.4	0.238
OSHIP KMIX	4	1	4	0.1	0.749
Explained	3858	10	385	9.3	0.001
Residual	3619	88	41		
Total	7477	98	76		

TABLE 6.9   *Multiple classification analysis (K79 by OSHIP M, A, B, KMIX)*

Grand Mean = 28.92 Variable and category	Unadjusted deviation	Eta	Adjusted for independents deviation	Beta
OSHIP				
Public	−7.8		−5.3	
Stock	2.3		1.7	
Mutual	−0.7		−0.7	
		0.37		0.26
M				
Direct	−18.8		−15.6	
Agents	0.4		0.3	
		0.31		0.26
A				
Established	−1.5		−1.5	
Young	10.9		10.9	
		0.47		0.46
B				
All	0.3		0.2	
Civil Servants	−7.6		−4.0	
		0.18		0.09
KMIX				
Kleinleben	5.5		6.0	
Normix	−1.1		−1.2	
		0.28		0.30
Multiple R squared				0.50
Multiple R				0.70

TABLE 6.10   *Analysis of variance (BK/79 by OSHIP M, A, B, KMIX)*

Source of variation	Sum of squares	DF	Mean square	F	Significance of F
Main effects	1425	6	237	9.9	0.001
OSHIP	490	2	220	9.1	0.001
M	163	1	163	6.8	0.011
A	15	1	15	0.6	0.435
B	38	1	38	1.6	0.214
KMIX	472	1	472	19.6	0.001
Two-way interactions	116	4	29	1.2	0.315
OSHIP A	12	1	12	0.5	0.481
OSHIP B	106	2	53	2.2	0.116
OSHIP KMIX	0	1	0	0.0	0.889
Explained	1541	10	154	6.4	0.001
Residual	2119	88	24		
Total	3660	98	37		

TABLE 6.11　*Multiple classification analysis (BK75/79 by OSHIP M, A, B, KMix)*

Grand mean = 15.78 Variable and category	Unadjusted deviation	Eta	Adjusted for independents deviation	Beta
OSHIP				
Public	−6.62		−5.52	
Stock	1.62		1.37	
Mutual	−0.08		−0.10	
		0.42		0.35
M				
Direct	−10.32		−9.20	
Agents	0.21		0.19	
		0.24		0.22
A				
Established	−0.16		−0.15	
Young	1.15		1.08	
		0.07		0.07
B				
All	0.22		0.13	
Civil servants	−5.11		−3.06	
		0.17		0.10
KMIX				
Kleinleben	6.01		5.21	
Normix	−1.16		−1.00	
		0.43		0.38
Multiple R squared				0.389
Multiple R				0.624

TABLE 6.12　*Analysis of variance (S79 by OSHIP M, A, B, KMIX)*

Source of variation	Sum of squares	DF	Mean square	F	Significance of F
Main effects	326	6	54	11.7	0.001
OSHIP	62	2	31	6.6	0.002
M	13	1	13	2.7	0.103
A	196	1	196	42.2	0.001
B	0	1	0	0.0	0.852
KMIX	28	1	28	6.0	0.016
Two-way interactions	64	4	16	3.4	0.012
OSHIP A	44	1	44	9.5	0.003
OSHIP B	9	2	4	1.0	0.390
OSHIP KMIX	26	1	26	5.6	0.020
Explained	390	10	39	8.4	0.001
Residual	409	88	5		
Total	798	98	8		

TABLE 6.13 *Multiple classification analysis (S79 by OSHIP M, A, B, KMIX)*

Grand mean = 5.26

Variable and category	Unadjusted deviation	Eta	Adjusted for independents	Beta
OSHIP				
Public	−1.96		−1.24	
Stock	0.87		0.76	
Mutual	−0.58		−0.67	
		0.35		0.28
M				
Direct	−4.01		−2.55	
Agents	0.08		0.05	
		0.20		0.13
A				
Established	−0.54		−0.54	
Young	3.89		3.93	
		0.51		0.51
B				
All	0.04		−0.01	
Civil servants	−0.98		0.20	
		0.07		0.01
KMIX				
Kleinleben	0.82		1.27	
Normix	−0.16		−0.25	
		0.13		0.20
Multiple R squared				0.408
Multiple R				0.639

TABLE 6.14 *Analysis of variance (GR79 by OSHIP M, A, B, KMIX)*

Source of variation	Sum of squares	DF	Mean square	F	Significance of F
Main effects	22	6	4	5.9	0.001
OSHIP	2	2	1	1.6	0.203
M	0	1	0	0.1	0.778
A	15	1	15	24.3	0.001
B	0	1	0	0.3	0.602
KMIX	2	1	2	3.4	0.070
Two-way interactions	3	4	1	1.3	0.262
OSHIP A	0	1	0	0.6	0.433
OSHIP B	1	2	0	0.7	0.509
KMIX	2	1	2	2.5	0.120
Explained	25	10	3	4.1	0.001
Residual	55	89	1		
Total	81	99	1		

TABLE 6.15　*Multiple classification analysis (GR79 by OSHIP M, A, B, KMIX)*

Variable and category	Unadjusted deviation	Eta	Adjusted for independents deviation	Beta
Grand mean = 6.73				
OSHIP				
Public	−0.30		−0.39	
Stock	0.04		0.07	
Mutual	0.04		0.03	
		0.12		0.16
M				
Direct	0.26		0.16	
Agents	−0.01		−0.00	
		0.04		0.03
A				
Established	0.15		0.15	
Young	−1.12		−1.09	
		0.46		0.45
B				
All	−0.01		−0.01	
Civil servants	0.22		0.21	
		0.05		0.05
KMIX				
Kleinleben	0.53		0.35	
Normix	−0.10		−0.07	
		0.26		0.17
Multiple R squared				0.273
Multiple R				0.522

TABLE 6.16　*Analysis of variance (BEGM by OSHIP M, A, B, KMIX)*

Source of variation	Sum of squares	DF	Mean square	F	Significance of F
Main effects	1177	6	196	0.4	0.873
OSHIP	405	2	202	0.4	0.659
M	37	1	37	0.1	0.782
A	661	1	661	1.4	0.246
B	54	1	54	0.1	0.739
KMIX	6	1	6	0.0	0.914
Two-way interactions	262	4	66	0.1	0.969
OSHIP A	73	1	73	0.2	0.698
OSHIP B	82	2	41	0.1	0.918
OSHIP KMIX	159	1	159	0.3	0.568
Explained	1440	10	144	0.3	0.980
Residual	40614	84	483		
Total	42053	94	447		

TABLE 6.17   *Analysis of variance (UE79 by OSHIP M, A, B, KMIX)*

Source of variation	Sum of squares	DF	Mean square	F	Significance of F
Main effects	80	6	13	1.6	0.171
OSHIP	15	2	8	0.9	0.418
M	3	1	3	0.4	0.545
A	44	1	44	5.1	0.027
B	0	1	0	0.0	0.848
KMIX	12	1	12	1.5	0.230
Two-way interactions	49	4	12	1.4	0.230
OSHIP A	19	1	19	2.2	0.140
OSHIP B	31	2	16	1.8	0.165
OSHIP KMIX	0	1	0	0.0	0.940
Explained	129	10	13	1.5	0.152
Residual	655	77	9		
Total	784	87	9		

measures the quality and the amount of information provided to the insured before purchase. If insufficient or misleading information is provided by agents, then early contract cancellation may be necessary, usually with substantial losses to the insured. Thus, the significantly higher S79 value for stock companies is an indication of bad service.[17] The complaint index shows no significant difference with respect to ownership, even though the mean complaint index BEGM of public enterprises is 1.3 as compared to 8.6 for stock companies and 6.3 for mutual companies.

With respect to other firm variables one further result deserves mentioning. Civil servants seem to have the same propensity to complain when compared to the remainder of the population. The four companies exclusively insuring civil servants do not deviate from average performance as measured by the reported indicators. In particular, the quality of service indicator, number of complaints per market share, is not significantly different for these firms.

Finally, we allowed for marked share, which has an insignificant impact on cost (at the 7 per cent level of significance). Hence, economies of scale cannot be substantial over the range of observed firm sizes. All the above relationships continued to hold when market share was allowed for.

CONCLUSION

The main purpose of the government intervention in insurance markets has been to prevent bankruptcy and to establish market transparency. Bankruptcy has been prevented, but market transparency is low. Even worse, certain regulatory policies ultimately cause intransparency. Into this category falls the *ex ante—ex post* profit regulation in the automobile insurance market and the strangulation of price competition in the life insurance market.[18]

The lack of market transparency reduces competitive pressure. This is why significant differences between the performance of stock companies, mutual companies and public enterprises may persist. Public enterprises and mutual companies seem to out-perform stock companies. For example, public life insurance companies produce at 24 per cent less cost than stock companies. Since they do not enjoy any tax preferences, it has been argued that their mostly regional structure may account for this cost advantage. If this were true, from a normative viewpoint all companies should stop their nationwide service and concentrate their operations regionally. If there was effective competition in this market other firms, in particular firms with expense ratios typical for the current market, would not survive.

NOTES

1. I am grateful for helpful comments from D. Bös, D. Farny, P. Kleindorfer, J. Müller, S. Peltzman, F. Schneider, C. C. v. Weizsäcker and from the regulation group at the Sonderforschungsbereich 21 of Bonn University.
2. See Prölss, E. R., R. Schmidt and J. Sasse (1978), p. 11.
3. Average rate of return on 'visible' assets of liability insurance companies were 42.8 per cent in the period 1974–9.
4. For details see F. M. Scherer (1980), p. 29.
5. Since 1960, only three firms entered the market for automobile insurance; twelve life insurance firms are less than ten years old. Today we find approximately one hundred firms in each market.
6. Note that neither mutual companies nor public enterprises enjoy tax privileges.
7. See Prölss, E. R., R. Schmidt, J. Sasse (1978), p. 289.
8. Note, $x(p, q)$ denotes the sales function of an individual firm in an industry with many firms. In an industry with one firm, a monopoly, this argument does not hold.
9. Some objections have been raised against the use of this index. First, it is argued that the propensity of customers to complain could be systematically related to the choice of firm type. Second, it is unclear which aspects of

quality the complaints refer to. In J. Finsinger and E. J. Flöthmann (Feb. 1981) we analyze the subset of complaints which were classified as justified by the regulatory agency. The pattern shown in Table 6.4 only becomes more pronounced. We also analyze subsets of firms with different specialization and obtain similar results.

10. It is generally acknowledged that the output per premium is largest for mutual companies who show a slightly higher loss record.
11. The cost ratios do not include the administrative cost of claim settlements, which on average amount to 8 per cent of premiums.
12. In fact, very few interesting performance indicators can be exactly determined from publicly available data. Only the regulatory agency knows the relevant data, but it does not publish material pertaining to individual firms. Only aggregate data is reported, which is of little interest for consumers. Business magazines have to estimate most indicators.
13. See *Capital* 10, 1980, p. 117.
14. Stock companies which are daughters of mutual companies are classified as mutual.
15. Daughter companies of mutual companies are classified as mutual companies even though they are set up as stock companies.
16. Those who wonder why a life insurance contract may still be a profitable investment should recall that the returns are exempted from taxation.
17. Note that the cash value of contracts with stock companies is lower than the cash value of contracts with public enterprises or mutual firms for the entire period of the contract, in particular at early cancellation.
18. Not all regulatory policies decrease market transparency. Many regulations of contractual clauses seem to be beneficial.

REFERENCES

Finsinger, J. (1981) 'Wettbewerb im Versicherungswesen – Die Kraftverkehrsversicherung'. *Wirtschaft und Wettbewerb (Journal of Competition and Trade Regulation)*, April, pp. 251–63.

Finsinger, J. and E-J. Flöthmann (1982) 'Rechtsformbezogene Leistungsunterschiede der HUK- und Sachversicherer', *Zeitschrift für öffentliche und gemeinwirtschaftliche Unternehmen*, vol. 5, no. 1, pp. 17–30.

Joskow, P. L. (1973) 'Cartels, Competition and Regulation in the Property-Liability Insurance Industry', *Bell Journal of Economics*, 4 (2), pp. 375–428.

Prölss, E. R., R. Schmidt and J. Sasse (1978) 'Versicherungsaufsichtsgesetz', *Kommentar*, 8 (München: Auflage).

Scherer, F. M. (1980) *Industrial Market Structure and Economic Performance*, (Chicago, Ill: Rand McNally).

7 An Economic Analysis of Law-Suit Insurance

MICHAEL ADAMS

The aim of this paper is to provide an analysis of the effects of law-suit insurances. About 42 per cent of households in the Federal Republic of Germany own such an insurance. The total value of the premiums paid in 1980 exceeded 1.7 billion DM. This rapidly expanding business is coming under increasing attack from persons working in the legal sector. The reason for these attacks is their belief that the availability of such insurances is the principal cause of the huge increase in the number of law-suits. The rapid rise in the number of civil processes has led to the formation of increasingly long waiting lists. They constitute a threat to the functioning of the legal system and the President of the German Federal Court of Justice (Bundesgerichtshof) has already referred to these time lags as amounting to a denial of justice.[1]

A systematic analysis of the functioning of law-suit insurances first requires an explanation as to why intelligent human beings decide to undertake expensive legal actions against each other. While the arguments to be presented here are formulated mainly in terms of civil law-suits it should be clear that the resulting analysis can easily be applied to other types of law-suits. This chapter first explains why parties decide to undertake law-suits and then analyses the significance the costs of the processes have on the decision, allowing consideration of the welfare implications of law-suit insurances.

THE DECISION OF THE PARTIES TO UNDERTAKE A LAW-SUIT

The basic assumption underlying this analysis which is common to practically all of economic theory, is that the parties engaged in a law-suit

134

do so because they hope to increase their own welfare. The decision of each of the parties whether to start a law-suit rather than accept a settlement outside the courts, must then result from the comparison of the benefits to be derived from each of these possibilities. Each party decides for itself, whether it finds it preferable to accept a settlement outside the courts, or whether it can expect a greater level of utility from starting a law-suit. The fact that intelligent people *do* decide to enter a law-suit may seem somewhat surprising at first sight, because a civil law-suit is a pure distributional fight (zero-sum game). As a result of the high costs of this fight, it would obviously be in the joint interest of the parties involved had they been able to come to an agreement outside the courts. The first problem that has to be solved is thus to find an explanation of why the parties fail to reach an outcome which is in their common interest. In order to make the exposition that follows as lucid as possible, the rest of this chapter discusses the payments and incomes that result from the law-suit and thus refers to the costs and benefits of the law-suit in purely monetary terms. It should be clear, however, that these monetary expressions are intended to reflect the utilities of the two parties.

The decision of the plaintiff to go to court

If a person believes that he has a claim against another person he will decide to go to court provided he expects to reach a higher income by going to court than by agreeing to some extraneous settlement which the opponent offers.

The fundamental structure of the decision problem of the plaintiff is determined by the fact that the outcome of the law-suit will only become known at some future date and is thus inherently *uncertain*. The plaintiff has to form some expectation about this future outcome. In order to describe the mechanism leading to this expectation let me introduce the following notation.

$E_k =$ the expected value of the law-suit as viewed by the plaintiff;

$p_k =$ the subjective probability, as viewed by the plaintiff, that he will win the process;

$G =$ the payment expressed in DM made by the defendant to the plaintiff, should the latter win the suit;

$K =$ the total costs of the process (that is, the costs of the lawyers of *both* parties plus the court costs of both parties).[2]

In order to reach an intelligent decision a person faced with uncertainty about the future will have to determine the number of

possible future outcomes and weight these with the subjective probabilities of occurrence. In the case of a law-suit the outcomes are either
victory or defeat. (Settlement during the process will not be explicitly
analyzed in this model, though its influence can easily be determined by
applying the same basic analysis. The lawyers with their better knowledge of the law can exert a strong influence on the parties' subjective
expectations and thus on their willingness to agree to a settlement.)

The economic value a risk-neutral[3] plaintiff will associate with a law-
suit is equal to its expected value. The plaintiff will receive an income of G
in case of victory, and will have to pay the total costs of the law-suit K in
case of defeat. The expected value of the law-suit is thus equal to

$$E_k = p_k \cdot G - (1 - p_k) \cdot K$$
$$E_k = p_k (G + K) - K$$

In a simple numerical example, the expected value of a law-suit, where
the amount disputed is equal to 10 000 DM, and the costs of both
lawyers and the court are equal to 3600 DM, the expected income of the
plaintiff is equal to

$$E_k = p_k \cdot 10\,000 - (1 - p_k)\, 3600$$
$$E_k = p_k \cdot (13\,600) - 3600$$

If, for example, the plaintiff is certain of winning and excludes the
possibility of losing, his subjective probability of winning (p_k) takes the
value of 1. The expected value of the law-suit is thus equal to

$$E_k = 1 \cdot 13\,600 - 3600 = 10\,000$$

Consider now a less certain situation where the plaintiff is uncertain of
winning and associates a probability p_k of only 0.5 to the outcome that he
will win. The expected value of the law-suit is then equal to

$$E_k = 0.5 \cdot 13\,600 - 3600 = 3200$$

The *expected value* of the process is of fundamental importance
because it determines the *minimum amount* the plaintiff would have to be
offered in order to accept a settlement outside the court. Should the
defendant be unwilling to offer this amount, the plaintiff will definitely
decide to go to court as the expected value of following this strategy

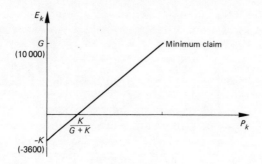

FIGURE 7.1

exceeds that of accepting the settlement-sum (which is lower). This is true in spite of the fact that he has a chance of losing and will then have to bear the total costs. Figure 7.1 shows how the minimum amount the plaintiff will have to be offered changes as a function of his subjective probability of winning. One can clearly see that the expected value of the law-suit and thus the minimum claim the plaintiff will make increases linearly with his subjective probability of winning and reaches the value of G only when p_k is equal to 1. Only when p_k is equal to 1 will the minimum claim be equal to the total value of the amount being disputed.

The decision of the defendant to enter a law-suit

The defendant will determine the economic value of the law-suit in an analogous fashion. He will also, in the case of risk-neutrality, determine the expected value the law-suit has for him and thus fix a lower limit for the amount he will agree to in a settlement outside the court. The defendant will not have to pay anything in case of a victory. In case of defeat he will have to pay both G and the total costs K. The expected value of the law-suit for him is thus equal to

$$E_b = p_b \cdot 0 - (1 - p_b) \, G + K$$

$$E_b = p_b \, (G + K) - G - K$$

In the example where the value disputed was 10 000 DM, and the costs amounted to 3600 DM, the (absolute) expected value for the defendant is then $|E_b| = (1 - p_b) \cdot 13\,600$. Should the defendant believe that he has an

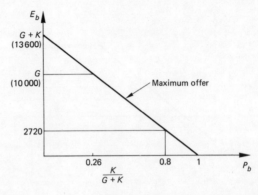

FIGURE 7.2

80 per cent chance of winning, his expected value is equal to

$$E_b = -(1-0,8)\,13\,600 = -2720$$

Thus the defendant will not be willing to agree to any payment in an outside court-settlement which exceeds 2720 DM. He will prefer going to court rather than paying an amount exceeding 2720 DM in spite of the costs and the risks involved in pursuing this strategy. The *expected value* for the defendant is thus the *upper limit* to the amount the defendant will offer the plaintiff in a settlement outside the court.

Figure 7.2 shows how the expected value of the law-suit to the plaintiff changes as a function of his subjective probability of winning.

Law-suit or settlement outside the court

Once both parties have determined their minimum claim and their maximum offer the circumstances under which a law-suit will result are apparent. A necessary and sufficient condition for a law-suit is *that the minimum claim of the plaintiff exceeds the maximum offer of the defendant,* that is

$$E_k > |E_b|$$

Consider again the example when the costs are of 3600 DM and the disputed sum is 10 000 DM. If both parties believe that they have 50 per cent chance of winning, the expected value to the plaintiff is equal to 3200 DM, for the defendant it amounts to 6800 DM. In the negotiations

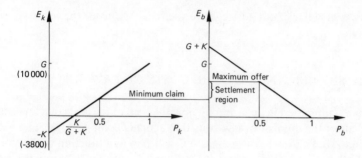

FIGURE 7.3

the plaintiff will fix his minimum claim at 3200 DM, the defendant has a maximum offer of 6800 DM. There is thus a range of 3600 DM, in which the parties can come to an agreement.

This is further clarified when Figures 7.1 and 7.2 are superimposed on each other (Figure 7.3).

If, however, the plaintiff were to believe that he has a 90 per cent chance of winning while the defendant stays with his 50 per cent chance the expected values are $E_k = 8640$ DM and $E_b = 6800$ DM. The minimum claim exceeds the maximum offer by 1840 DM and a law-suit is unavoidable. This is graphically illustrated in Figure 7.4.

When the difference (ΔE) between the minimum claim E_k and the maximum offer $|E_b|$ is positive

$$\Delta E = E_k - |E_b| > 0$$

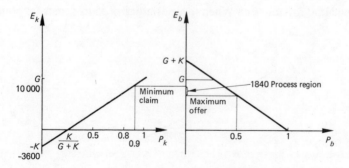

FIGURE 7.4

a law-suit will result. If it is negative a settlement outside the court will be reached.

THE SIGNIFICANCE OF THE COSTS OF LAW-SUITS

If one is interested in determining how the level of the costs of a law-suit will effect the number of law-suits that actually come to court, one will have to study how the difference, ΔE, will vary as a function of the level of K. Substituting the equations for E_k and E_b into the equation for ΔE one obtains

$$\Delta E = (p_K + p_b - 2) K + (p_K + p_b - 1) G$$

$$d(\Delta E)/dK = p_K + p_b - 2$$

With the exception of the extremely rare case where both parties are certain of winning, any increase in costs will lead to a decrease in the number of disagreements which actually are brought to court. Again this idea can be illustrated using the numerical example above. Suppose that in the law-suit for 10 000 DM the plaintiff believes he has a 90 per cent chance of winning, while the defendant believes he has 80 per cent chance of winning. This gives a difference between the minimum claim and the maximum offer (ΔE) which is equal to

$$\Delta E = -0.3 K + 7000$$

Once again Figure 7.5 illustrates that – given these probabilities of winning – when the legal costs are zero then there will be a gap between the highest offer and the lowest claim which is equal to 7000 DM, and this will lead to a law-suit. When the legislator introduces costs for going

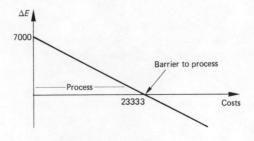

FIGURE 7.5

to court, the gap between the offer and the claim decreases by 300 DM for every 1000 DM increase in costs, so that the claim would just exactly equal the offer when the costs reach 23 333 DM. The parties will then settle outside of court.

This consideration clearly indicates that the legislator can, by fixing the level of legal costs, influence the number of disputes that actually do appear at the court. The higher the costs the greater must be the difference in the parties' subjective expectations of winning before a law-suit can result. It follows that any institution which reduces the costs of going to court for one or both of the parties, such as Government subsidies for the courts, law-suit insurances and so on, will necessarily lead to an increase in the number of law-suits.

We may conclude that *the subjective expectations of the parties as well as the costs of court are an inseparable part of any subjective right.* It is thus impossible to separately analyze material law without explicitly taking into account the effect of uncertainty and legal costs. Any factor that changes the legal costs or influences the parties' subjective expectations alters the parties' material rights. Thus, a claim for 1000 DM which a party holds according to material law does not have any value to that party, even with a 90 per cent chance of winning, if the costs of a law-suit exceed 9000 DM, as his expected value is equal to

$$E_k = 0.9 \cdot 1000 - 0.1 \cdot 9000 = 0$$

If, however, it were possible for him to go to court without having to fear the resulting costs, the expected value of the claim would equal 900 DM.

This observation is of fundamental importance for the analysis of law-suit insurances.

THE EFFECTS OF LAW-SUIT INSURANCES

A law-suit insurance policy enables its holder to undertake law-suits without fearing the resulting costs. The insurance company will pay the legal costs, both in the case of defeat and in the case of settlement. These costs include the costs of lawyers, of courts, of experts and of witnesses and so on.

Let us first assume that only the plaintiff can go to court without fearing any cost, while the defendant has to bear the risk of these costs. Graphically we have Figure 7.6. Any reduction in the costs makes the idea of going to court a more attractive alternative.

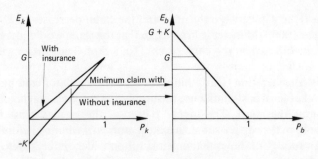

Fɪɢᴜʀᴇ 7.6

Fɪɢᴜʀᴇ 7.6

It follows immediately that a party free of costs will reduce its willingness to accept a settlement outside the court. As there does not seem to exist any sensible rule determining where the parties will end up within the interval of settlement one can use the principle of insufficient reason and expect that the actual outcome of the settlement will be a stochastic symmetrically distributed function in the interval between the minimum offer and the maximum claim. The actual average settlement will then just lie in the middle of the interval. It then follows that the party which is free of legal costs will obtain a pecuniary gain as result of increasing its minimum-claim. The level of this gain is equal to the loss which the party would have had to accept had it reduced its maximum claim as a result of legal costs. As we have assumed that the difference between the minimum-claim and maximum-offer is evenly distributed among the two parties, the average gain in case of a settlement outside the court is equal to one half of the increase in the minimum claim or one half of the decrease of the maximum offer. Any increase of 1 DM in the minimum claim which the party gains as a result of not having to cover its own costs will lead to a gain of 0.50 DM in case of a settlement outside the court. The same is true for the decrease of the maximum offer of 1 DM.

For the *welfare analysis* of the effects of law-suit insurances, it is important to note that the gain of one party is just exactly equal to the loss of the other as the law-suit is a pure distributional fight (zero-sum game). It would thus be wrong and misleading to analyze the effects of a one-sided reduction in legal costs by considering only this one party without taking into account the effect this will have on his behaviour towards his fellow men, and, in particular, the reduced willingness to come to a peaceful agreement which results directly from the reduction in his costs. It would be even more erroneous to analyze the effects of this cost reduction by considering only those cases where the dispute is actually carried to court. Rather, what is important for the understanding of the effects of this cost reduction is the fact that the party whose costs have been reduced can reduce its willingness to settle and thus make the described gain at the expense of his fellow men *without* actually ending up at court. It could then be the case that a party which is free of legal costs never actually has to go to court, but can nevertheless earn huge profits by being less transigent in a large number of cases. The purchase of such a cost reduction can be compared to the acquisition of a pistol. The gain resulting from the acquisition of a pistol is given by the sum of cases in which a victim is threatened and has nothing to do with the number of shots actually fired. An intelligent criminal can (given a sufficiently incompetent police force) become rich as a result of using a weapon as a threat without firing a single shot.

One can conclude that a one-sided reduction in costs for one party will lead to an unambiguous redistribution of income away from the party which has to carry its costs to the benefit of the party which is freed of its costs. When a party succeeds in being freed of its legal costs it has imposed a loss on all of the parties with which it is in potential conflict, who are not in possession of the same cost advantage. This results directly from the decreased willingness to settle. A party which is freed of its costs has effectively acquired a weapon to obtain a redistribution at the expense of its fellow men. This means that the material law has changed simply by a reduction in legal costs without any change in the text of the law. If, however, the law has been devised for a given system of legal costs by a legislator who was aware of their implication, then any change in the system of costs which was not wanted by the legislator should be considered a welfare loss. Whether the redistribution of legal right results from a change in the law itself or a redistribution of the costs is of little importance given the inseparable link between them. While a citizen cannot simply change the word of the law he can nevertheless alter its effects by acquiring a law-suit insurance, thus obtaining a cost advantage. This has the effect of distorting the law and that has the same welfare effects as a change in the law itself. We may thus conclude that an asymmetric reduction in the costs of going to court will lead to a welfare-decreasing redistribution in the content of material rights at the expense of those individuals who have to carry their own costs. However, the *effects of a cost reduction* do not exhaust themselves with this welfare decrease which results from the *redistribution of rights*. The reduction in the willingness to come to an agreement will lead to an *increase in the number of law-suits*. Given that the subjective expectations of the parties are independent of the level of costs, the reduction in costs will automatically lead to an increase in the sets of combination of subjective probabilities which will lead to a law-suit. If one is willing to accept that the level of legal costs is fixed at their welfare-maximizing level, then the introduction of the possibility of costless legal processes will lead to a welfare-reducing increase in the number of law-suits.

However, this one-sided reduction in the costs of law-suits which results from the existence of law-suit insurances cannot, in the long run, be a stable situation.

The gains made by the insured result from their increased ability to threaten their uninsured fellow men. These will react by insuring themselves to obtain a counter threat. The resulting equilibrium (Nash equilibrium) is welfare-inferior for all concerned. The reason is as follows: the acquisition of a tool for threatening somebody is of value only as long as the threatened person does not himself acquire an equally effective counter threat. Once both parties have armed themselves their relative position is unchanged but they are worse off to the extent of the cost they have incurred in arming themselves. They would have done better to forego the temptation to threaten and exploit each other. This is the sad story of the armaments race.

This chapter ends with a short description of this 'armaments race' and the resulting *equilibrium*.

Let us first start off with a situation in which all the parties have to bear the risk of the costs except for one individual who has acquired a newly created law-suit insurance. This one party, which no longer has to fear any costs, will harden its bargaining position and make the redistributional gains described above. The uninsured parties will realize that their position has worsened and notice the benefits to be gained from a law-suit insurance. It gives them the possibility of hardening their bargaining position and defending themselves against the individual who is already insured. They also will insure themselves. This reaction by the uninsured parties has unfortunate consequences. The party which started the process cannot retrace its steps, leave the insurance and reinstate the original situation. It now has to fear being exploited by the parties who bought insurances as a result of its own threats. Even those who started off by using the insurance as an aggressive measure will have to remain insured for defensive reasons. The gains and costs of a law-suit insurance in a dynamic 'armaments race' of all citizens can be described as follows.

When the percentage of uninsured individuals in the population is low there is a gain to be made by insuring oneself and thus improving the conditions one can obtain in settlements outside the courts. These benefits are earned at the expense of the non-insured citizens. When the share of the insured individuals rises this will lead to an increase in the number of law-suits among them. It does not seem reasonable in this general analysis to suppose that the distribution of the settlement and process area, which resulted from the inconsistent expectations of the parties, is systematically distorted in favour of the plaintiff or the defendant. It seems more reasonable to assume that, not only the distribution of the settlement area, but also the distribution of the process area by the courts, is stochastically symmetric. If the parties have thus opened, by their expectations, a process area, this process area will not necessarily be distributed systematically in favour of one of the parties; any distribution of the process area by the courts, it is assumed, has the same probability of happening. This means that the resulting distribution does not depend on the fact of settlement or law-suit. If a person has thus the possibility of increasing his minimum-claim as he has no costs to bear, he always makes a certain gain, which is independent of whether the reduced willingness to settle causes a process or a settlement. The size of the gain is thus independent of whether the parties go to trial or succeed in a settlement. The increasing number of law-suits caused by the increasing percentage of insured persons does therefore not influence the *gains* resulting out of a law-suit insurance. The private gain of having a law-suit insurance is thus independent of the number of insured persons within a society.[4]

The opposite is true for the *costs* of a law-suit insurance, that is, the *premium-change* over time. The possibility of starting a law-suit free of marginal costs reduces the readiness to settle and increases the number of law-suits. The greater the number of individuals who are insured, the greater will be this effect. The costs of this increased number of processes must, however, be borne by the insurance companies and thus, indirectly, by the insured. The greater the number of law-suits per insured individual, the greater the average costs and the higher will be the premiums. As the benefits of becoming insured remain constant, while the premiums rise with the number of insured individuals, an equilibrium (at x^*) will be reached where a given percentage of the populations is insured. This equilibrium x^* is illustrated in Figure 7.7. At that point the marginal benefits of being insured are exactly equal to the level of the premiums.

This raises the question what *welfare properties* one may expect from this *equilibrium*.

First note that there is still a non-insured section of the population

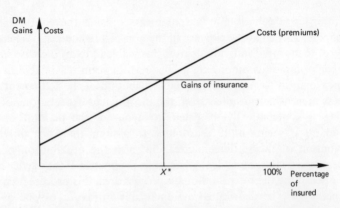

FIGURE 7.7

that loses a part of its rights as a result of the insured individuals'
greater ability to threaten. This *redistribution* leads to a welfare loss as
well as an *allocative inefficiency of civil law.* The material rights of the
individuals are changed. Furthermore, the equilibrium has the property
that the lower willingness to reach a settlement will cause a large increase
in the *number of law-suits.* The number of settlements outside the courts
which the legislator had initially hoped for is not reached and a large
resource-consuming number of law-suits is carried to court. The insured
individuals themselves will, in equilibrium, have to carry a large part of
this cost increase in the form of higher premiums. One may thus
conclude that the *law-suit insurances* are of *benefit to none* but *do damage
to all.*

NOTES AND REFERENCES

1. Pfeiffer, G. (1978) 'Rechtsfriede and Rechtsschutz durch Richterspruch',
   Gesprächskreis Politik und Wissenschaft, Friedrich-Ebert-Stiftung.
2. It should be noticed that the German civil law-suit regulations state that the
   party that loses the law-suit has to bear the total costs of *both* parties caused
   by the law-suit. The loser has to pay not only his own lawyer and witnesses but
   also the court fees and the total costs of his adversary.
       Furthermore, it should be mentioned, that the lawyers' fees are also
   regulated by binding law. The fees are a degressively increasing function of
   the disputed sum. The regulation consists of a binding minimum-fee law,
   which leaves the lawyer only the right to demand higher fees, but not offer his
   services at a cheaper price. But the defeated party, who has to pay the costs of
   the winner, has to pay only the minimum fees. In practice these are also the
   prices that most lawyers charge.

In a very simple law-suit the lawyer may charge only the simple fees. They are doubled, if the case is personally disputed before the courts, and the fees are tripled, when it becomes necessary to hear witnesses. The maximum price of four times the basic fee is reached when the lawyer succeeds in reaching a settlement within the courts, after the previously mentioned steps have already been taken. The settlement fees explain the common fact that about 40 per cent of all civil law-suits end with settlement and not with a decision by the court. The lawyers attain this high settlement percentage by influencing the subjective probabilities of the parties involved, who generally do not know the lawyers' incentives for settlement.

3. In Adams, M. (1981) *Ökonomische Analyse des Zivilprozesses* (Athenäum Verlag) the author extensively analysed the effects of risk aversion, in particular 'constant relative risk aversion', which requires the introduction of subsidies for the poor to prevent civil law-suits leading to a redistributional effect against the poor. Furthermore, the allocation efficiency of the law is disturbed by the existence of such redistributive effects of constant relative risk aversion.

In the present context it is sufficient to point out, that the existence of risk aversion works to increase the effects resulting from the existence of law-suit insurances.

4. It should be mentioned that the above welfare results remain essentially true if the assumption that the process area is equally distributed among parties is changed such that the gain of an insured decreases with the percentage of the insured population. A stable equilibrium will still exist. This would be even true if this gain increases with the percentage of insured at a rate not exceeding that of the rise in premiums.

Part IV
Pharmaceutical Industry

8 Price Regulation in the European Pharmaceutical Industry: Benefits and Costs

HORST-MANFRED SCHELLHAASS and ULRICH STUMPF[1]

INTRODUCTION

Currently, three approaches to drug pricing may be identified in EEC countries:[2] relying on market forces (West Germany, the Netherlands and Denmark), regulating profits (UK) and regulating individual drug prices (France, Italy, Belgium/Luxemburg, Greece and Ireland[3]).

So far, economic studies on EEC drug markets have examined competitive behavior and regulatory interventions from a national point of view. But the research-intensive part of the drug industry operates on a multinational level. Only in West Germany and the Netherlands do the market shares of foreign-owned companies not exceed 40 per cent (see DAFSA, 1977, p. 67). World-wide marketing has been a vehicle to earning supra-normal profits in the 1950s and 60s; due to the higher costs and risks of research and development (R&D) it is becoming a necessity. Schwartzman (1976, pp. 143–9) has estimated on the basis of (1972 US) research costs, that a new chemical entity will earn over 10 per cent (after taxes) on the investment in research only if annual world sales exceed $m 23.5. Even providing for lower research costs in EEC countries, no national drug market in Europe is able to support sufficient sales.

The question of 'who pays for European drug research' arises.[4] Clearly, national regulatory schemes must be seen as a means of limiting

151

the national contribution to R&D investment undertaken by multi-national companies. We will present the regulatory approaches and discuss their impact on the intra-EEC allocation of R&D costs. A number of price comparisons appeared in the mid-seventies, suggesting that intra-EEC price differentials may be related to regulatory interventions; we will briefly sketch the evidence.

Though short-run benefits of regulations may be attractive from a national point of view, long run costs must not be neglected. Regulation leads to an allocation of R&D resources to socially less productive alternatives. Moreover, a reduction in global contributions reduces the amount of resources devoted to R&D of new chemical entities. Regulators should take into account that a reduction in the rate of therapeutic advance prevents potential welfare gains in both regulating and non-regulating countries.

SHORT-RUN BENEFITS OF REGULATION

The National Aspect: Reducing the Drug Bill

From a distributional point of view the pharmaceutical industry is criticized for several reasons. It is widely believed that imperfections on the demand side[5] are the main reason for the 'excessively' high price–cost margins of modern drugs.[6] Indeed, the accounting profit rates of the pharmaceutical industry lie considerably above the average industrial level (see Grabowski and Mueller, 1978, p. 332). It is further believed that competition does not work properly in the drug market because price competition is widely absent and barriers to entry as well as intense advertising restrain potential competition. Under these circumstances regulation is considered necessary to limit profitability in the pharmaceutical industry to a competitive level. Regulation would lead to a more equal distribution of industrial profit rates and to the transformation of a producer's into a consumer's surplus, which would ease the heavy financial problems of the social security systems or national health services.

The International Aspect: Beggar-my-Neighbour Policy

As all research-intensive pharmaceutical firms are multinational enterprises, a regulating country may reduce its share of common R&D costs at the expense of other countries. This is depicted for the simple one

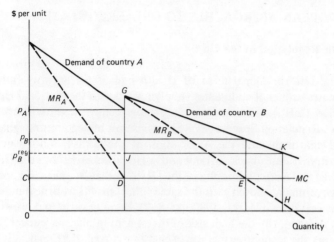

FIGURE 8.1

product – two countries case in Figure 8.1. The enterprise maximizes its short-run profits if it discriminates prices for its patent protected drug.[7] The equalization of marginal revenue (MR) with marginal costs (MC includes the opportunity costs of capital in multi-product firms) leads to quantity CD and price p_A in country A and quantity DE and price p_B in country B. Let us now assume that country B regulates the price to p_B^{reg}. This changes the marginal revenue function in B from GEH to JKH. The comparison of the opportunity costs of further delivery (= marginal production costs because the research costs for this drug are sunk costs by now) with the reduced earnings yields the optimal short-run reaction of the firm to price controls. As long as the regulated price still yields a positive contribution to the R&D costs, the regulating country will be further provided with the drug. This condition is generally given for the cost structure of modern drugs.[8]

Thus, regulation generates short-run reductions of the domestic drug bill, as the regulated country obtains a drug of the same quality, but at a lower price and in a higher quantity than previously. These potential benefits may be one of the reasons why some EEC member states regulate the prices and profits of pharmaceutical firms. The different regulatory schemes that have emerged in Europe will briefly be discussed in the following section.

EUROPEAN APPROACHES TO DRUG REGULATION

Profit Regulation in the UK

In the UK the Department of Health and Social Security (DHSS) regulates profits of companies supplying drugs to the National Health Service (NHS). The underlying arrangement – the Pharmaceutical Prices Regulation Scheme (PPRS) – is a result of negotiations between the Department and the Association of the British Pharmaceutical Industry. It dates back to 1969 and was revised in 1972 and 1978.[9]

The regulatory philosophy of the DHSS is that 'supplies of goods to the government should earn the same sort of profits as British industry in general does' (Marks, 1980, pp. 8, 9). Because of (i) the growth of drug demand, (ii) the high risk of investment in pharmaceutical R&D and (iii) the accounting method of charging current R&D expenditures, accounting rates of return in the pharmaceutical industry have been well above the average level in manufacturing industry (see Schwartzman, 1976, pp. 155–60). Regulating profits down to average levels in the UK amounts to a refusal to share the incurred costs and risks of pharmaceutical R&D with unregulated markets. It ignores that in the growth stage of an industry life-cycle with high risks of investment, above-average profits are perfectly justified, since they attract the necessary resources to serve demand. But constraining profits is attractive since it reduces the NHS share of global contributions to investment in R&D[10] and generates a short-run increase in UK welfare. Company returns submitted to the DHSS (since 1967) show that the average profitability of UK exports has been constantly above the average profitability of the NHS home trade.

The Pharmaceutical Price Regulation Scheme states that, when judging profitability, the DHSS should take account of 'the contribution which the company makes or is likely to make to the economy, including foreign earnings, investment, employment or research'. Acquiring the sponsorship responsibility from the Department of Trade and Industry, the DHSS discriminates between companies according to their capital basis in the UK. Clearly, UK companies (with most of their research and production facilities established in the UK) may be able to earn higher profits compared to foreign firms with little more than a sales organization in the UK.[11] Consequently, DHSS offers some sharing of costs and risks with unregulated markets, if investment is undertaken in the UK.

Drug prices in the UK will continue to react to market conditions, since a company is able to shape its price structure within its profitability constraint. In unregulated markets new (patent-protected) drugs are introduced with skimming or penetration price strategies, depending on the degree of therapeutic novelty and on company expectations of future innovations. Reekie (1977) found that UK regulation had no impact on the choice of price strategies for new products. Though a profit constraint will reduce a companies price level, the price structure of its line of products will remain intact.

Product Price Regulation in France, Italy and Belgium

France, Italy and Belgium/Luxemburg[12] are relying on statutory price controls for drugs whose costs are reimbursed by the national Social Security funds. Prices of new drugs are regulated on the basis of cost calculations or price comparisons.

According to the *French* regulations the degree of therapeutic advance of a new drug has to be assessed by a commission of the Securité Sociale. If the drug represents no therapeutic advance, it will be accepted as reimbursable only if it is priced below the prices of existing substitutes. If the drug is of superior therapeutic quality, the commission may accept a higher price.[13] Reimbursement of accepted drugs may be cancelled if new drugs of at least comparable quality but lower price are introduced. This provides for a constant pressure to match lower prices of new drugs. The French government frequently orders price freezes, rarely interrupted by global price increases. Since accepted price increases hardly compensate for cost inflation, the level of French contributions to investment in pharmaceutical research has been well below those of unregulated countries.

Moreover, maximum price calculations on the basis of costs (abolished in 1980) led to an extensive discrimination against foreign-based firms: (i) R&D costs were accepted in the calculations only if they originated in France, (ii) royalties for drugs licensed by foreign firms were restricted to 5 per cent of the maximum price and (iii) transfer prices for chemical substances imported from foreign parent companies were strictly regulated in order to prevent inclusion of R&D contributions. Therefore, companies marketing drugs developed and produced in France were granted higher prices. Whether the new regulations will be handled in a less discriminatory way is uncertain, since criteria for determining maximum prices of new drugs are less specific.

Surprisingly, the number of new products entering the French market has been higher than in non-regulating countries. Since accepted price increases did not match cost inflation, older drugs were withdrawn. They were replaced by new drugs whose chemical structure was slightly modified (which generally represented no therapeutic advance), but whose maximum prices took cost inflation into account.[14] Since the new regulations no longer provide for cost calculations, there might be less interest in slight molecule structure modifications in the future.

Companies are prevented from shaping price structures according to market conditions. They are no longer able to opt for skimming price strategies (with the possible exception of significant therapeutic advances) or for a strategy of keeping high contributions per unit after patent protection expires (reallocating resources as the product's market share declines).

Italian regulations provide for maximum price determination of new drugs on the basis of cost calculations. Price comparisons for imported drugs were abolished in 1977. Previously, prices of imported drugs were restricted to the price of locally produced equivalent drugs or (in the absence of local production) to their respective prices in the exporting country (plus transfer costs).

Regulations currently in force in *Belgium (and Luxembourg)* provide a number of criteria which may arbitrarily be applied by the ministry of trade. They include price comparisons with identical drugs in other countries or with similar drugs in the Belgian market, cost calculations, contributions of the regulated company to the Belgian economy, and so on.

Clearly, Italian and Belgian regulations can be used to reduce the national contributions to R&D, but since both schemes provided for foreign price comparisons in the past, they should have been less discriminatory. Because prices of drugs imported to Italy (Belgium) were pegged to the price in the exporting country until 1977 (1975), there was some sharing of R&D contributions, if the exporting country was not regulating prices.[15] The new Italian regulations rest on cost calculations with strict constraints on transfer prices of chemical substances imported from foreign parent companies and on royalties for licensed drugs. Belgian price controls, in force since 1975, take domestic investment, employment and exports into account, discriminating against companies with a smaller capital basis in Belgium.

To sum up, regulation in some EEC countries is used to constrain the domestic share of global contributions to investment in therapeutic progress. It rests with unregulated markets to bear the bulk of R&D costs and risks. Moreover foreign suppliers are discriminated against since their profitability and prices are constrained according to their capital basis and research in the regulating country. Allocative distortions are worst in the case of price regulations since companies try to achieve a higher price level via increasing product differentiation.

Price Differentials in the European Community

A number of price comparisons appeared in the mid-seventies. They show that (in 1974) the unregulated German prices were on average well above the regulated UK, French and Italian prices. Although price comparisons on the basis of drugs common to two (or more) countries are subject to a number of criticisms,[16] Table 8.1 presents rather consistent evidence.

TABLE 8.1 *Relative prices for drugs common to West Germany and the UK, West Germany and France, and West Germany and Italy (West Germany = 100), 1974. Conversion with 1974 exchange rate*

	Kiel study*	Prognos study†	Cooper study‡
United Kingdom	54.1	69	55
France	60.4	59	52
Italy	77.4	75	–

* Prices at manufacturer's level; SOURCE Glismann and Seusing (1975, p. 184).
† Prices at manufacturer's level; SOURCE Prognos (1976, p. 76).
‡ Prices at chemist buying level; SOURCE Cooper (1975, pp. 8, 12; own calculations).

Since we are interested in national contributions to R&D investment of companies marketing new drugs on an international level, conversion of national price levels with 1974 exchange rates seems to be a reasonable measure. A parent company's revenue from foreign markets increases (decreases) if the exchange rates of respective foreign currencies increase (decrease). If prices are converted with exchange rates current for the year in question, German prices steadily rose versus UK, French and Italian levels over the six-year period, 1970–5. Note that Italian prices were still above the German level at the beginning of the seventies. The increasing price differentials can be explained to a large extent by the revaluation of the German Mark against the pound Sterling, the Franc and the Lira. Table 8.2 shows that if prices are converted throughout with the exchange rate ruling in 1970, French and

TABLE 8.2   *Relative prices (at manufacturing level) for drugs common to West Germany and UK/France/Italy (West Germany = 100), 1970–75. Conversion with exchange rates current for the year in question, and 1970 exchange rate*

	1970	1971	1972	1973	1974	1975
West Germany–UK						
current exchange rates	90	84	76	66	69	68
1970 exchange rate	90	86	84	87	98	110
West Germany–France						
current exchange rates	77	72	70	65	59	61
1970 exchange rate	77	75	73	72	72	70
West Germany–Italy						
current exchange rates	126	121	112	94	75	73
1970 exchange rate	126	125	119	120	110	113

SOURCE   Prognos (1976, pp. 76, 86).

Italian prices decline to a lesser extent while UK prices increase against the German level. Obviously, one should be cautious relating changes in relative prices (converted with current exchange rates) to changes in the intensity of competition or in the strictness of regulatory control. But, since market structure in EEC drug markets is not too dissimilar, a constantly lower price level can be related to regulation. It seems that regulation is an efficient means for an international income redistribution – at least as long as the non-regulating countries pay for the total R&D costs. But in the long run we must expect that research-intensive enterprises react to price controls by changing their *future* product mix, which means that the distributional effects of regulation can only be realized at an economic cost.

LONG-RUN COSTS OF REGULATION

The Impact of Regulation on the Innovative Competition

We turn now to the analysis of the role of R&D in explaining above-average profit rates. As the long-run profit rates do not equal the competitive rate of return on capital, the pharmaceutical industry must have been able to erect some 'barriers to entry'.[17]

We first consider the patent system as an entry barrier. The high degree of empiricism of pharmaceutical research has the consequence that an important portion of technical progress is due to the attentive observation of a lucky hit. But the more inventions are found by chance, the less the innovator is able to explore systematically the neighbourhood of a new chemical entity and to fence in his inventions by patents. Therefore the patent system is a relatively unreliable barrier to entry. For almost all new chemical entities substitutes are found by rivals during the patent-protected period of the original invention. Thus, the existence of patent protection cannot satisfactorily explain the above-average profit rates of the pharmaceutical industry.

Usually, economies-of-scale barriers have been postulated to arise from R&D because investment in it is costly, risky and subject to economies of specialization and scope. Undoubtedly, economies of scale require a certain minimal optimal scale for R&D to be undertaken efficiently. Although these factors might operate to produce above-average returns, these could be competed away by vigourous intra-industry rivalry in R&D activity.[18]

Moreover, if the hypothesis of the economies-of-scale barrier is correct, regulation should not divert resources from the R&D sector, because 'fair' price controls still allow a competitive rate of return. In the traditional limit-price model, taxing away the supranormal profits should only have distributional effects. This is a question which can be answered empirically. Case studies of the pharmaceutical industry (for example, Grabowski, 1976, pp. 17–38, or Reis-Arndt, 1978) show that R&D regulations have reduced both the number of ineffective or effective but unsafe new chemical entities.[19] This is a clear indication that taxing away innovational profits has distributive as well as allocative effects. This result rules out the possibility of economies of scale limit-price profits. For a comprehensive analysis we have to look for an alternative explanation of the nature and function of barriers to entry in innovative industries.

If chance plays an important part, a successful R&D activity not only requires the written – and thus transferable – scientific knowledge; what is also needed, is a special kind of intuition to detect the incalculable chance. Thus, the R&D capacity of a pharmaceutical firm is an intangible capital stock composed of knowledge, experience and tradition, which needs many years of continuous R&D to achieve its full capacity.[20] It is here that the R&D divisions of newcomers are at the greatest competitive disadvantage.

In all research-intensive industries potential entrants have to consider the possible outcome that they are second in the innovative competition. That means either a lower price or a smaller market share in comparison to the innovator's one, or – worst of all – a ruinous cut-throat rivalry from the established firm.[21]

In the pharmaceutical industry the risk of being unsuccessful and losing the non-recoverable R&D costs is significantly higher than in other industries because it is very difficult for a newcomer's inexperienced R&D division to try to keep up with the established firms for the initial product as well as in the future technological race. Successful entry would require either a pathbreaking innovation – which is a rare event – or an equivalent innovation linked with the ability to develop an advanced succeeding product in accordance with the short product cycle of the industry. The innovator can increase the problems of potential competitors through short product cycles. This requires on his side the introduction of advancements before rivals have caught up with the technology incorporated in the present products. The innovator shapes the market structure by constantly trying to be technologically ahead of his rivals. In this way he can capture the innovational profits and earn an above-average rate of return, and simultaneously increase the problems of newcomers to such an extent that they do not try to enter.

The underlying barriers to entry are based on fast technological advance (short product cycles) in connection with the important role of chance in pharmaceutical research (the aquisition of the necessary experience takes several years, which equals a competitive disadvantage). They are very different from economies-of-scale entry barriers. We call them *dynamic barriers to entry* because they are exposed to erosion.[22] As the development of equivalent drugs is relatively easy due to the high degree of empiricism in pharmaceutical research (patent protection is weak), the firms have to re-invest the greater part of their high profits in new R&D activities to secure high profitability in the future through the lucrative sale of advanced drugs. Contrary to the conventional barriers to entry, we find, for the dynamic ones, that the private advantage of a high rate of return is linked with the social advantage of a high rate of innovation.

If dynamic barriers to entry are the main reason for the above-average rates of return, price controls will change the incentive structure of a pharmaceutical company in the long run. R&D projects are usually selected according to the same cost–benefit criteria as normal investments in productive capacity; that means the present value of the expected returns has at least to be equal to the present value of the expected costs (including a reasonable risk premium).[23] The risk of a future price control is reflected by a regulatory risk premium which is equivalent to the present value of the expected losses of revenues compared to free competition (Eads, 1980, p. 53). This regulatory risk premium reduces the benefit–cost ratio of all planned R&D activities.

Thus, under regulation, the interest of fast technological advances dwindles to the extent that price controls change the benefit–cost ratio of innovations towards the negative. As a consequence the pharmaceutical firms cut down their R&D budgets and the rate of pharmacological progress declines.

Regulation and the Optimal Investment in R&D

Hirshleifer and Riley (1979, pp. 1403–6) cite several reasons for a market failure with respect to optimal investment in R&D. Two of them seem to be especially relevant for the pharmaceutical industry.

> Due to the high degree of empiricism, patent protection is relatively weak, and even in strong patent positions the owner cannot impose perfectly-discriminating royalty fee structures on licensees, so we cannot exclude an underinvestment in *path-breaking* innovations (see Arrow, 1962).
> On the other hand, there is strong evidence that innovative competition leads to an exaggerated product differentiation, which means that the market gives too many pecuniary incentives to engage in *substitutive* R&D activities. Reducing the capturable value of the invention itself might moderate an excessive 'rush to invent' (see Hirshleifer, 1971, pp. 569–72).

The pharmaceutical research process is largely a process of screening thousands of chemical substances in search of some potential beneficial therapeutic properties. Given the screening technology, most inventions result from some sort of molecular manipulation. An inventive company may end up finding an important therapeutic novelty. Therefore, we can think of therapeutic advances and 'me too' inventions as joint products, resulting from the same R&D process.

Ex ante, it is almost impossible to draw a line between research for important therapeutic novelties and speculative research in search of 'me too' drugs. If we are concerned with waste of resources resulting from 'me too' inventions, we should bear in mind that they are the price for therapeutic progress. The optimality problem is then simply: what price should society pay for therapeutic advances in terms of 'me too' innovations? Of course, the price may be too high, as R&D productivity declines and the ratio of 'me too' inventions to important novelties increases as the industry enters maturity. In that case, regulation would increase welfare. However, intervening at an earlier stage would divert resources from pharmaceutical R&D, preventing potential welfare gains.

Also, regulation reduces the contributions to the R&D costs per period such that a budget equilibrium can be achieved only through a longer economic life of the drugs. This requires a more effective protection of the existing products against potential rivals. In a regulatory environment the innovator can extend the life of his outstanding products by making competitive entry more difficult through the production of a whole product line. Under these circumstances the innovator himself intensifies product differentiation. While under free market conditions the R&D division conquered new unknown territories in order to secure the dynamic barriers to entry and thus the above-average profit rate, price controls induce a defensive R&D policy which seeks to maintain the given market position.

CONCLUSION

Dynamic barriers to entry do not imply a distortion in the allocation of resources, but they have an economic function. We observe that there exists an optimal intertemporal structure of rates of return over the life cycle of a product or industry: an above-average rate of return in the growth stage is followed by a normal rate of return in the stage of maturity and by a below-average rate of return in the stage of stagnation. Thus, the rate of return differentials have the economic function of providing monetary incentives for shifting resources from stagnating to growing industries. In this way, the intertemporal structure of rates of return facilitates the continuous change of economic structures.[24] In other words, a regulated equalization of industrial rates of return would aggravate the structural problems of the economy.

A positive side effect of dynamic barriers to entry is that they disappear more or less as soon as the innovative activity declines; this happens when the pharmaceutical industry enters the stage of maturity. This leads to the result that even if the government refrained from all interventions, above-average rates of return would eventually disappear. As an industry will enter the stage of maturity with certainty, economic policy makers could be in a lucky position with respect to dynamic barriers to entry. Thus, the distributional gains of regulation are limited to the growth stage of the pharmaceutical industry.

But while the regulating country gets all the short-run gains, the costs of regulation, namely the lower rate of pharmaceutical discovery and innovation, have to be shared by all countries (the 'echo' effect of regulation, Grabowski, 1976, p. 23). The regulating country takes advantage of the uniform rate of pharmaceutical innovation at the expense of those countries which pay their full competitive contribution. The less countries control their prices, the higher is the expected ratio of benefits to costs (the advantage of the 'small' country in international trade theory). Due to the asymmetric distribution of costs and the benefits of price controls there is little hope that politicians will voluntarily desist from this modern form of the beggar-my-neighbour policy. Presumably this kind of international distributional struggle can only be restrained by international agreements between governments.

NOTES

1. We are greatly indebted to Jörg Finsinger for suggestions and criticisms of an earlier draft.
2. See also Schwartzman (1979) for a recent treatment.
3. Only if drugs are locally produced.
4. We will not discuss the allocation of research costs between EEC and US or Japanese markets or the question of supplying developing countries.
5. The incentive system does not work in the normal manner because the physician prescribes, the patient consumes and the health insurance pays for the drugs.
6. The variable costs of the tranquillizer Valium for example are 4 per cent of producer's price; see the decision of the German Federal Cartel Office in the Valium–Librium case, p. 88.
7. Intra-EEC price differentials should – if large enough to cover transfer costs – attract arbitrage on the retail level. So far, arbitrage has almost been non-existent due to (i) high transfer costs, (ii) national registration regulations and (iii) the use of industrial property rights to separate markets. Since (regulated) pack sizes differ widely from country to country, arbitrageurs have to repack drugs and provide them (in Germany and France) with the local manufacturer's information for patients. Importers have to obtain marketing approval by the registration authorities. These have not been granted in a number of countries if arbitrageurs were not able to supply the full registration documentation on pharmacological and clinical tests. And finally, manufacturers used nationally granted industrial property rights (patents, trademarks) to prevent parallel imports of their drugs. The European Court of Justice has clarified the legal issues in a number of cases. National registration authorities have to approve imported drugs if the manufacturer already obtained a marketing approval in the importing country. Failure to do so amounts to a restriction of intra-EEC trade, which is an infringement of Article 30 of the EEC Treaty (Centrafarm, 1976). In an earlier case (Sterling Drug vs. Centrafarm, 1974), the Court of Justice ruled that an arbitrageur may import goods patented in

one member state for sale in another member state where they are also patent-protected. Moreover, an arbitrageur may use the manufacturer's brand name in the importing country (Hoffmann La Roche vs. Centrafarm, 1976), even if it is different from the manufacturer's brand name in the exporting country (American Home Products vs. Centrafarm, 1976). Nationally granted industrial property rights must not be used to separate EEC markets (which again is an infringement of Article 30 of the EEC Treaty). Since the legal issues are clarified by now, there may be some arbitrage activity at the retail level in the future, but for the moment, arbitrage is still widely absent.

8. This explains why even sales to those countries with the stiffest price regulation are not stopped – for example, Greece.

9. Regulation in the UK began in 1957 on the basis of price controls. Maximum prices were based on (i) the average export price, (ii) the price of therapeutically equivalent generics (unbranded drugs) or (iii) on a cost calculation. Instead of applying maximum price formulas, firms as well as the DHSS could opt for direct negotiations on drug prices, taking into account the overall profitability of the companies' NHS trade. The Sainsbury Report (1967, p. 30) estimates that in 1964/65 50 per cent (by value) of proprietaries were already covered by direct negotiations. The introduction of a new scheme in 1969 only amounted to a standardization of a procedure already in use.

10. The reduction in contributions may be achieved by (i) lower prices, (ii) cash rebates to the NHS or (iii) free or low-priced hospital supplies to the NHS.

11. The Department provides for some adjustment, (i) since profits earned in the NHS trade are to be related to a capital basis which may include part of the capital invested in foreign countries and (ii) since research costs in other countries may be charged against UK profits to the amount of the share of NHS sales to global sales (weighted with NHS prices) (See Scott-Moncrieff, 1976, p. 11). Moreover, foreign companies may include R&D contributions in the transfer prices of imported chemical substances.

12. We will not elaborate on Greek and Irish price controls.

13. Since cost calculations (statutory demanded since 1948) were abolished in 1980, the underlying criteria for maximum price determination of superior new drugs are not quite clear. Cost calculations of drugs representing no therapeutic advance were already replaced by price comparisons in 1977.

14. 21.1 per cent of all new drug entities discovered 1961–77 were first marketed in France (Germany 14.2 per cent, UK 9.9 per cent, Italy 7.6 per cent, Benelux 4.3 per cent, USA 8.0 per cent). France is only second to the US in the number of new drug entities by country of invention, 1961–77 (US 23.4 per cent, France 19.3 per cent, Germany 12.6 per cent, Italy 7.0 per cent, UK 5.1 per cent, Benelux 2.7 per cent). (See Reis-Arndt, 1978, pp. 6, 8.)

15. This problem is obviously seen by the British authorities: if prices in UK export markets are pegged to UK prices, the DHSS may be prepared to accept higher UK prices in order to ensure a higher export revenue and thus higher R&D contributions both in the UK and export market.

16. Choosing drugs common to two countries may result in comparing apples with pears (i) if common drugs have widely dissimilar market shares in their therapeutic submarket or (ii) if the relevant therapeutic submarket has a

dissimilar share of the total market. We may end up with comparing different stages of maturity in (i) the product cycle or (ii) the sub-market cycle.

17. Von Weizsäcker (1980) has pointed out in a recent article that the traditional use of the term 'barriers to entry' does not allow the conclusion that they are a distortion of the competitive process. He proposes a revision in the definition such that the term is restricted to those 'barriers to entry' which imply a distortion in the allocation of resources from the social point of view. This proposition acknowledges that the inefficiency connotation of the concept is by now deeply ingrained in the use of the term by policy-oriented economists.

On the other hand we have a similar problem in pollution policy. Not all emissions of a firm imply a distortion in the allocation of resources; nevertheless we use the same term for the socially allowed and the socially detrimental emissions. By analogy, we stick to the Stigler definition of barriers to entry because it is used traditionally in the industrial organization literature. We are aware, however, that we can only draw welfare or policy conclusions from it after having made a cost–benefit analysis.

18. It is nearly impossible to keep outlays on innovational activity at joint profit-maximizing levels even within highly concentrated industries.

19. The cited case studies refer to the effects of the Kefauver–Harris Amendments of 1962. Though they impose more stringent registration rules which increase the costs of R&D projects, they are comparable with the European price regulation schemes with reference to the *rate* of technical progress. In both cases the profitability of R&D projects is negatively influenced. The result is indifferent to whether the earnings of the innovations are reduced by a certain amount (price controls in the EEC) or the costs of the innovations are increased by an equivalent amount (admission rules in the USA). Admission costs can be passed in part to consumers by increasing prices. The amount to be compared with the loss of revenues is not equal to the increased admission costs but to the net loss of profits. Price controls and admission rules differ, however, with respect to the *direction* of pharmacological advance.

20. A part of this ability is embodied in a few scientists of the incumbent firm and thus difficult to acquire by outsiders.

21. Even if the rival is not less efficient than the innovator, he has no chance to win if the innovator chooses an entry-deterrent pricing strategy: assuming an identical remaining life for both products, the innovator has always the possibility of undercutting the competitor's prices because he has to allocate the smaller amount of R&D costs over the remaining life of the products. He has already earned a certain amount of reimbursement during the first years when he monopolized the market. These initial earnings form the economic basis for the innovator to enter eventually into a cut-throat rivalry with the entrant which is destructive for the latter. This is the risk of coming second in the innovative competition.

22. While, once erected, economies-of-scale entry barriers yield lasting limit-price profits, dynamic barriers to entry yield only supra-normal profits as long as the company offers better-than-average products.

23. As far as the innovative activity is governed by profit expectations, we must

analyze the demand-pull factors if we want to explain why, and in which manner, pharmaceutical companies react to regulation. Our reference system is the time path of innovative activity in a free market economy. If however the *total change* of the rate of technical progress within a given time period is to be explained, we have to take account of demand-pull factors as well as technology-push factors.

24. From an allocational point of view, interventions are justified when the rate of return differentials are higher than is necessary for the desired change of economic structures.

REFERENCES

Arrow, K. J. (1962) 'Economic Welfare and the Allocation of Resources for Invention' in: *The Rate and Direction of Inventive Activity* (Princeton, NJ: Princeton University Press) pp. 609–25.

Cooper, M. H. (1975) *European Pharmaceutical Prices* (London: HMSO).

DAFSA (1977) *L'Industrie Pharmaceutique en Europe* (Paris).

Eads, G. C. (1980) 'Regulation and Technical Change: Some Largely Unexplored Influences', *American Economic Review*, 70, pp. 50–4.

Glismann, H. H. and E. Seusing (1975) 'Probleme internationaler Preisvergleiche–Pharmazeutische Produkte', *Die Weltwirtschaft*, 2, pp. 176–90.

Grabowski, H. G. (1976) *Drug Regulation and Innovation, Empirical Evidence and Public Policy Options* (Washington DC: American Enterprise Institute for Public Policy Research).

Grabowski, H. G. and D. C. Mueller (1978) 'Industrial Research and Development, Intangible Capital Stocks, and Firm Profit Rates', *Bell Journal of Economics* 9, pp. 328–43.

Hirshleifer, J. (1971) 'The Private and Social Value of Information and the Reward to Inventive Activity', *American Economic Review*, 61, pp. 561–79.

Hirshleifer, J. and J. E. Riley (1979) 'The Analytics of Uncertainty and Information – An Expository Survey', *Journal of Economic Literature*, 17, pp. 1375–421.

Marks, D. S. (1980) 'The Cost of Health Care Systems – A Government View' (unpublished manuscript).

Posner, R. A. (1975) 'The Social Cost of Monopoly and Regulation', *Journal of Political Economy*, 83, pp. 807–27.

Prognos, (1976) *Internationale Markt- und Preisvergleiche im Pharmabereich* (Basel:).

Reekie, W. D. (1977) *Pricing New Pharmaceutical Products* (London).

Reis-Arndt, E. (1978) *Neue pharmazeutische Wirkstoffe, 1961–1977*, Pharma Dialog Nr. 57, Bundesverband der Pharmazeutischen Industrie.

Schwartzman, D. (1976) *Innovation in the Pharmaceutical Industry* (Baltimore: Johns Hopkins University Press).

Schwartzman, D. (1979) 'The Regulation of Drug Prices', in: G. Teeling-Smith and N. Wells (eds), *Medicines for the Year 2000* (London: Office of Health Economics) pp. 42–56.

Scott-Moncrieff, W. (1976) 'Operation of the UK Voluntary Price Regulation Scheme', *SCRIP*, 5 June, pp. 10–11.
von Weizsäcker, C. C. (1980) 'A Welfare Analysis of Barriers to Entry', *Bell Journal of Economics*, 11, pp. 399–420.
Decision of the German Federal Cartel Office in the Valium–Librium case: *Wirtschaft und Wettbewerb* (1975) 25, pp. 84–102.
Report of the Committee of Enquiry into the Relationship of the Pharmaceutical Industry with the National Health Service, 1965–67 (1967) (Sainsbury Report) (London: HMSO).

9 Price Comparisons of Identical Products in Japan, the United States and Europe

W. DUNCAN REEKIE

INTRODUCTION

This chapter reports on a study of eight leading multinational pharmaceutical firms each of which markets products in Europe, the United States and Japan. One motivating factor behind the exercise was that, increasingly, governments and academics have resorted to international price comparisons to ascertain whether or not a given firm's price range or a given product's price was 'fair' (NEDO 1972; Cooper, 1975). Second, no such comparison with the methodology used here has been carried out before.

PREVIOUS STUDIES

Earlier work in this area has either been restricted to one product, or to an unrepresentatively small number of products, (Monopolies Commission, 1973; Royal Canadian Commission on Health, 1964, pp. 677–9); or, alternatively, to virtually all products available in a given control country (usually the UK) for which comparable products were available elsewhere (Cooper, 1966). This latter approach appears to have the virtue of total comprehensiveness. But, in fact, from a total of 2500 products available in Britain only 79 important products (by British sales value) could be directly compared with their, in this instance, German equivalents. This figure fell to 42 when a comparison was made between the British and Italian markets (Cooper, 1966, p. 122). Moreover, since the Cooper studies (1966, 1975) used the UK as a base from which to draw a sample, the resulting comparisons were of Britain with each of the other countries in turn. They were not juxtapositions of 'analogous drugs' in a range of countries.

Valier (1959; 1961) attempted to do this by restricting himself to six national markets and examining directly comparable drugs available simultaneously in each market. Only 18 products were deemed directly comparable, however, and a further 40 required standardization by either pack size or dosage before a price comparison could be made. As Cooper (1966, p. 141) pointed out 'the actual number of fifty-eight would not have mattered, given that they were the *right* fifty-eight, which is . . . highly improbable' (emphasis in original). Cooper was correct since, on a product basis, the pharmaceutical industry does not have a diffuse market structure. In most countries well over half of all sales by value are made by well under half the number of available products. At any point in time, however, the mix of the leading products, varies widely from country to country according to medical convention, disease incidence, legislative and commercial factors (Reekie, 1975, pp. 62–70). Thus to find even a small number of drugs common to all markets is not enough. The products must all be important in their respective markets. If they are *not* all commercially important products then any results calculated would be biased towards minimizing overall price differences. This is because, given the normal negative relationship between price and quantity, more relatively highly priced products would by studied (Frisch, 1947, pp. 21–36). Moreover, the products which contribute most to consumer satisfaction or medical care could thus be ignored in one or more countries.

In addition, product similarity and duplication may mislead the analyst. For meaningful price comparisons from which inferences can be drawn about national pricing practices, transfer price policies and the like, the marketing company must be the same (or have the same corporate parent). If it does not, then the wide variety of royalty and licensing arrangements which are possible can dramatically alter the prices which are charged. For example, this was the situation in the UK when Roche Products Ltd charged both Berk and DDSA Pharmaceuticals an absolute royalty based on weight of chemical sold, and not, as is more usual, a percentage of sales value achieved. This set a floor beneath which the licensees could not price and survive (Polanyi, 1973, p. 49). It was decided that a different approach could be justified in the present examination.

First, the 'comprehensive' approach of Cooper would not be repeated:

(1) since it had resulted in only a small number of product comparisons in any event;
(2) since the starting point for the sample design was the country (generally the UK) then the product juxtapositions were of each country with the available drugs in Britain, not of each country's analogies.

Second, the 'analogous drug' approach of Valier was rejected because, again, the starting point was the country rather than the firm or the product. This resulted in product comparisons between a small number of not necessarily important products.

Moreover, there is a wide variety of marketing methods for pharmaceuticals by country and their fiscal treatment is also varied. For example, in the USA a high proportion of medicines are paid for directly by the general public (albeit after prescription by a doctor). The price paid by the public will depend on what the manufacturer's selling price was, what wholesale margin was levied, what retail margin was obtained by the dispensing chemist and what level of sales tax was raised at each stage of the distributive process. At each stage these will influence what the 'price' is. They will vary state by state (in the case of taxes) and possibly even transaction by transaction in the case of discounts awarded or gained.

In Europe, Nelson (1980) has shown that the mark-ups levied by wholesalers, retailers and the national tax authorities can range from

TABLE 9.1 *Trade margins on price paid by public (including national taxes – price paid to manufacturer by wholesaler = 100)*

Austria	154	Finland	83
W. Germany	111	France	80
Denmark	110	Sweden	78
Norway	100	Belgium	77
UK	98	Spain	65
Eire	94	Italy	58
Switzerland	88	Greece	43
Netherlands	86	Portugal	43

SOURCE J. D. E. Nelson, 'International Price Comparisons', unpublished talk, American Management Association, Zurich, 1980.

154 per cent in Austria to 43 per cent in Greece and Portugal. His full
listing is given in Table 9.1. In addition, the 'price' ultimately charged to
the 'public' will vary with the method of financing of health care and the
presence or absence of resale price maintenance (RPM). In the UK the
monopsonistic National Health Service negotiates prices with the
industry through the Pharmaceutical Price Regulation Scheme, dispensing chemists reimbursement levels are fixed by government, and RPM –
or 'a fair trade law' – is in force. In other countries the public themselves
pay market-determined prices directly to the retailer to either a greater
or a lesser extent. RPM is not universal and the tax treatment of
distributors differs.

THE CURRENT STUDY

The present investigation examined prices at the level of the manufacturer. First, and most importantly, it is manufacturers' net receipts
about which governments and others are most universally concerned.
Second, the 'comprehensive' type of studies mentioned above examined
chemists' buying prices net of tax, but including wholesalers' margins.
Although valiant attempts were made to remove the complexities of the
tax factor, which varies not only internationally but in some cases
changes rate according to product price (NEDO, 1972 p. 19) the
problem of differing wholesale margins remained.

It was decided, therefore, to approach manufacturers directly and
obtain from them their selling prices, net of all taxes and wholesale and
retail margins. The eight companies selected for the sample were chosen
non-randomly solely on the basis of whether or not they would
cooperate in the provision of information. Of the eight firms who agreed
to assist there were representatives from Switzerland, Germany, the

TABLE 9.2   *Leading international pharmaceutical firms, 1970*

	Total world pharmaceutical sales ($m)	Average sales	Maximum	Minimum	Standard deviation
All Firms	9968	262	840	53	177
Sample Firms	2765	345	840	67	251

SOURCE   Extracted from the draft report of the Pharmaceuticals Working
Party, Economic Development Committee for the Chemical Industry
(a UK government body on which the author served).

UK, the USA and France. Each of the sample members are included in the top 38 pharmaceutical firms selling world-wide. Table 9.2 shows the sample is biased towards the larger firms in the population. It accounts for around 28 per cent of all world-wide sales.

The selling prices of the top five products of each firm were obtained for each of Japan, the USA, the UK, Germany, France and Italy. In each case the price obtained was for the most commonly sold pack size. The number of products (five) is arbitrary. However, as pointed out above, only a few leading products account for most of a company's sales. Von Grebmer (1978) calculated that in one European country 50 per cent of the ten leading firms' sales by value was accounted for by 5 per cent of their products by number. In the UK Reekie (1975, p. 127) found a similar situation. The leading twelve firms sold 526 products, but of these a mere 28 (approximately 5 per cent) accounted for 58 per cent of sales on average.

An absolute figure of five products, and those the top five products per firm, was therefore deemed to represent each company's major sellers. Clearly the number of products examined had a lower bounding figure of 40 and an upper bound of 240. However, although the same leading five products in one market were not always identical to the eight firms' five leaders in another of the six national markets, they did overlap to a considerable degree and the number of products studied was much closer to the lower than the higher figure. In fact, the total number of products examined was 56, and in the case of one firm only four product prices were obtained since only four products were sold commonly in the sample countries, and no other single product had significant sales in even one of the national markets examined. The raw data were collected by postal questionnaire and follow-up communications were made in each case where unexpected responses of this type (that is, information on only four products being obtained) cast initial doubts on the accuracy of the response.

PROBLEMS IN THE STUDY

Restrictions were placed on both the calculation and the presentation of the results. First, not all of the same products were sold in each of the sample countries. Thus comparisons had to be made between economic blocs in turn rather than with each of them simultaneously. This had to be done to maintain sub-sample comparability. Second, 'Europe' as an economic entity was restricted to four countries (the UK, France,

Germany and Italy) for similar reasons. Third, the data were only made available on condition that intra-European comparisons were not made public.

Some general problems of international price comparisons had also to be overcome. First, because of varying legal requirements and distributive mechanisms typical pack sizes sometimes vary immensely between markets. Thus in France and Germany pharmacists are compelled by law to dispense the manufacturer's original pack to the patient (to ensure that all relevant product information is passed on to him). In Japan, Italy, the USA and the UK this is not so. The product is broken up and repackaged in smaller amounts by the chemist. Thus French and German packs tend on average to be below the size of those in the other countries. Other things being equal, if prices are related positively to manufacturing and packaging costs, and if scale economies are present, then French and German prices will be higher than those for other countries. This difficulty can be partly overcome by calculating each price in per-unit terms (capsule, tablet, cream per gram, liquid per millilitre, ampoule and so on) and then, if the most commonly sold pack in any country is different from that sold in other countries, standardizing its price to that of the most frequently sold pack internationally. When this is done the French and German average price falls *vis à vis* the British, Italian and Japanese prices. The individual quantitative results cannot be shown here, given the conditions under which the data were supplied, but they did reflect what was intuitively expected.

Second, pack size standardization must also be carried out when, as often happens, the presentation of the product differs. (For example, in some countries a 125 mg capsule may be modal, in others the relevant presentation may be 250 mg units.) When this occurred the average price multiple for the product was applied.

Third, in some therapies the pack and the unit are often identical or nearly so. This is particularly the case with injectable ampoules. Ampoule prices are consequently 'high' when compared with the prices of other units such as tablets (which may be consumed by patients in lots of 25 or 100 per treatment, compared to the single unit dosage of an ampoule). It would be expected, therefore, that the average price per pack would generally be biased downwards relative to the average price per unit.

Finally, although the results are presented in index number form, no attempt was made to weight the products by sales per country. This omission was due to lack of data availability. It would have been possible to weight the products by therapeutic market size, as has been done by Cooper (1975). However, Cooper discovered that this made little difference to his conclusions. Of greater importance is the observation that weighting by sub-market sales (for example, weighting one antibiotic product by all antibiotic sales in a given country relative to all pharmaceutical sales) is only a proxy for normal index number weights. Indeed it is probably a poor and misleading proxy for the purposes of this study. Certainly it helps embody differing national medical practices or therapeutic requirements in the model (for example) antibiotics are relatively more frequently prescribed in northern than in southern Europe; for tonics and vitamin preparations the reverse is true).

TABLE 9.3   *Products in common between Japan and the USA (US price = 100)*

	(A) Japanese price per standardized pack	(B) Japanese price per dosage unit
(1) Price in dollars	206	228
(2) Price in minutes of work	231	254
(3) Price in 'effort units'	248	275
(4) Price in dollars deflated by GDP per capita	275	304
(5) Price in dollars deflated by physicians per capita	293	324

NOTES AND SOURCES   (See Table 9.6)

But in this study the differing morbidity patterns within Europe probably also occur, for similar climatic reasons to the USA. In addition, and most importantly, each of the products examined is a critical and major product to the company concerned. Thus to weight it by either its own sales or by its own sales plus those of its therapeutic market competitors in addition is somewhat redundant. The sample already consists of self-selected 'heavily-weighted' products both from the commercial viewpoint of the firm and from the viewpoint of the consuming nation. Trivial products in tiny market segments have already been excluded from the study by the nature of its sample design.

What is being compared are the prices of all the major products of a sample of major firms in the three largest drug markets in the world (Reekie and Weber, 1979, p. 28). The results are presented in Tables 9.3–9.6. A list of Notes and Sources is given after Table 9.6.

TABLE 9.4   *Products in common between the USA and Europe (European price = 100)*

	(A) US price per standardized pack	(B) US price per dosage unit
(1) Price in dollars	89	90
(2) Price in minutes of work	74	68
(3) Price in 'effort units'	65	65
(4) Price in dollars deflated by GDP per capita	78	78
(5) Price in dollars deflated by physicians per capita	90	91

NOTES AND SOURCES   (See Table 9.6)

TABLE 9.5   *Products in common between Europe and Japan (Japanese price = 100)*

	(A) European price per standardized pack	(B) European price per dosage unit
(1) Price in dollars	58	64
(2) Price in minutes of work	68	74
(3) Price in 'effort units'	65	72
(4) Price in dollars deflated by GDP per capita	50	59
(5) Price in dollars deflated by physicians per capita	40	44

NOTES AND SOURCES   (See Table 9.6)

RESULTS

The prices are calculated (in index number terms) in dollars per pack and in dollars per dosage unit at the ruling exchange rates as given in the 1980 *IMF Yearbook*. Subject to all of the previous discussion, Japanese prices appear to be approximately twice those of America (Table 9.3) and less than one half as high again as European levels (Table 9.5). This would imply that European prices are somewhat above those of the USA, as was found to be so (Table 9.4).

TABLE 9.6   *Products in common between the UK and Europe (including the UK)*
(European price = 100)

	(A) British price per standardized pack	(B) British price per dosage unit
(1) Price in dollars	92	100
(2) Price in minutes of work	112	122
(3) Price in 'effort units'	118	127
(4) Price in dollars deflated by GDP per capita	113	122
(5) Price in dollars deflated by physicians per capita	101	110

NOTES AND SOURCES
(1) GDP per capita computed from data in *IMF Yearbook, 1980, International Financial Statistics* (Washington: IMF, 1980).
(2) Exchange Rates and GDP per capita in US dollars as in note (1).
(3) Hours of work per week in all manufacturing industry and average earnings per hour in US dollars were taken from the *1979 Yearbook of Labour Statistics* (Geneva: ILO, 1979).
(4) Physicians per 10 000 population obtained from the *WHO Statistical Annual 1977* (Geneva: WHO, 1977).
(5) Earnings per 'effort unit' was computed by dividing earnings per hour (in dollars) by hours of work per week.
(6) Price in minutes of work was computed by dividing the product price by earnings per hour and multiplying by 60.
(7) Price in 'effort units' was computed by dividing product price by earnings per 'effort unit'.
(8) Relative prices adjusted by the relevant GDP and physicians per capita deflators are self-explanatory except in the case of Europe.
(9) The overall European prices used in Tables 9.4–9.6 were calculated using the simple arithmetic average of the national prices. This appears an acceptable approach given that the populations of the four nations were not dissimilar at 53, 56, 57 and 61 million for France, the UK, Italy and Germany, respectively. Similarly, for consistency the 'European' figure for GDP per head and physicians was obtained using the simple mean.

However, these figures depend on calculations made at international exchange rates and the simple purchasing power of money in its domestic environment does not necessarily explain its foreign exchange value. Yet in row (1) of Tables 9.3–9.6 foreign exchange values have been implicitly used to compare the purchasing power sacrificed by consumers to buy comparable products. Row (2) in each table attempts to overcome this by examining the prices in terms of minutes of work required to purchase the products. The disparity between American and Japanese prices grows in Table 9.3. This reflects the higher earnings per hour of the US worker. The European price disparity with Japan shrinks, since three of the countries (Italy, France and the UK) have hourly earnings well below those in Japan and the West German figure of $7.14 per hour is insufficient to offset the lower earnings in the other countries. The figures were $4.71, $4.06, $4.15 and $5.96 for France, Italy, the UK and Japan, respectively. For similar reasons, the British price *vis à vis* the European, rises in row (2) of Table 9.6, and this is despite the fact that the UK is included in both numerator and denominator of the index number calculation.

Earnings per hour is only one measure of income. It may simply reflect labour productivity differentials. Thus products could be 'inexpensive' in rich countries and relatively costly in those with lower productivity per hour. Moreover, in the six nations examined there was a 13 per cent spread in hours of work spent per week in manufacturing industry (lowest as a percentage of highest) with the UK and USA, for example, having average working weeks per head of 43.5 and 40.4 hours, respectively. If it is assumed that such figures would be little affected by the practice of 'moonlighting' or the holding of more than one full time job, since it is difficult for the average worker in an economy to adjust his total hours worked, some measure other than earnings per hour may be appropriate to calculate real income per head adjusted in some way for leisure time foregone. In this exercise 'earnings per effort unit' has been devised for this purpose. Since 'earnings per effort unit' (EPEU) equals earnings per hour divided by hours worked per week, EPEU will be smaller the longer the working week, other things being equal. In turn, if earnings per hour are higher in high productivity nations, but the working week is also shorter, then EPEUs for such countries will be larger still. Thus, when prices per EPEU are calculated the differential attributable to variations in the working week should be highlighted when these prices are compared with the equivalent prices expressed in minutes of work.

In row (3) of Table 9.3 the Japanese price in effort units rises still further in relation to the American price. This reflects the longer Japanese working week. In row (3) or Table 9.4 the price in the USA falls relative to the European price (reflecting the shorter working week in the USA relative to all European countries, except Italy at 38.5 hours). The similar average working week in Europe and Japan is such that the price differential indicated by comparing rows (2) and (3) of Table 9.5 is trivial. In Table 9.6, however, the longer British working week (relative to the European average including the UK) is such that the British price, measured in effort units, rises relative to the figures in rows (1) and (2).

Thus prices did change as casual observation might have suggested. America enjoys greater per capita productivity than the other economic blocs studied. Nonetheless the use of EPEU adjustments to prices measured simply in minutes of work does not result in major changes. US prices are lower than Japanese or European ones when measured by the latter technique. This may reflect productivity differences. But when the prices are recomputed using EPEUs, which explicitly embrace superior productivity, the US prices are adjusted still further downwards, albeit not dramatically. In rows (4) and (5) of each table the price in dollars in row (1) is modified by another measure of income per head, namely GDP, and one of welfare, namely physicians per capita in the population. GDP is an alternative to either hourly earnings or earnings per effort unit. Since it is not perfectly correlated with income received per head, and since in many countries pharmaceuticals are paid for either directly by the state or by patient reimbursement from the state or other bodies, then GDP may be a more appropriate price deflator than earnings received. In the case of physicians, not only are they an index of income or welfare, but pharmaceuticals by and large, cannot be sold without the presence of a prescribing doctor, irrespective of payment or reimbursement scheme.

As can be seen (from Table 9.3) the Japanese price rises again relative to the USA figure; Japanese GDP is less per head than American, and the market potential or welfare measure of physicians is only 11.6 per 10 000 population compared to 16.5 in the USA. In Table 9.4, row (4), the American price is seen to be a little lower than the unmodified dollar price due to Europe's slightly higher average GDP (mainly due to the West German GDP figure, but partly also to the French). The relative wealth of two countries in Europe in terms of physicians (19.4 and 19.9 for West Germany and Italy, respectively per 10 000 population) do little to change the US price in row (5), however. (Certainly France and the UK have equivalent figures of only 14.7 and 13.1.) In Table 9.5, the relatively high GDP figures per capita for Germany and France are partly offset by Italy and the UK's lower figures. In row (5) of Table 9.5, however, where all four European countries are better off in terms of physicians than Japan (at 11.6 per 10 000 population) the effect on the dollar price is more obvious, falling by around 20 points on either a pack or unit basis. The UK's relatively low GDP, like its other income measure, hourly earnings, results in a UK price in row (4), Table 9.6, almost identical to that in row (2). (Only Italy is below the UK in size of per capita GDP in the four European countries.) The UK, however, is relatively better off in terms of physicians per head than in terms of GDP per head and so in Table 9.6, row (5), the price indices fell back again to the figures shown.

Frequent and substantial changes in currency rates of exchange can make any price comparison between countries both obsolete and meaningless. For example, consider a product priced at a given monetary level in both the UK and West Germany in 1970 and assigned an index value of 100 in sterling terms. That same product would, if the money prices in each market remained the same, still have an index price of 100 in the UK. But in West Germany, if the unchanged Deutschmark price was converted into sterling on the 1st January, 1980 then it would be found to have a sterling index figure of 231. Thus in 1970 the products would appear to be identically priced. In 1980 the German price would appear to be more than double the British figure. Meanwhile the product itself had been subject to no monetary price adjustments in either market.

Tables 9.3–9.6 use exchange rate data from the 1980 *IMF Yearbook*. This makes for consistency in the calculations of GDP and GDP per capita which are based on data abstracted from the same source. To ascertain how sensitive the results are to using more recent exchange rate figures the price per pack in dollars is recomputed for each of Tables 9.3–9.6 and the outcome is presented in Table 9.7. The exchange rates used were those of early February, 1981 a date soon after the final questionnaire was returned and around one year after the exchange rates used in the main study.

How important exchange rate movements are in distorting results of the kind detailed in the main paper is highlighted in Table 9.7. Again the main conclusion is that interpretation of international price comparisons is a task fraught with difficulties and one from which only the pretentious would draw policy conclusions.

TABLE 9.7 *Dollar prices per pack calculated at exchange rates ruling in 1980 and 1981*

	1980	1981
(1) Japan (USA = 100)	206	243
(2) USA (Europe = 100)	89	104
(3) Europe (Japan = 100)	58	43
(4) Britain (Europe = 100)	92	101

As a consequence of the yen appreciating by around 18 per cent against the US dollar in the period examined the Japanese price ratio, relative to American products rose to 243. Not only did the dollar fall in value against the yen, it also did so against the pound sterling. However, each of the other European currencies fell against the dollar by more than offsetting amounts with a consequential apparent price increase in the USA *vis à vis* Europe to an index figure of 104. All European currencies fell relative to the yen (including the pound) and so the European price index number suffered the drop shown. Finally, the appreciation (around 5 per cent) of the pound (from \$2.22 to \$2.34) coupled with the more substantial falls in the value of the mark, the lire and the franc, (of around 20 per cent against the dollar in each case) resulted in the British price rising relative to the 'European' average.[1]

CONCLUSIONS

Irrespective of the exchange rate used or the measure adopted for calculating prices it appears that drugs in Japan are priced consistently higher than their European or American equivalents. The question is begged as to why this should be so. One can only speculate. It seems possible, however, given knowledge of the industry, that price controls are in many countries strict and rigid except in Japan. To the extent that governments hold down prices by suasion or dictat (and so presumably affect profits) in countries other than Japan, then there will be a movement of resources into pharmaceuticals in Japan, and a movement away from this industry in other countries. There is ample evidence of this latter trend (see, for example, Virts and Weston, 1980). Pharmaceuticals could thus follow shipbuilding and automobiles as victims of Japanese competition. There is no reason for disquiet about this if it is the result of genuine comparative advantage. If, however, it is the outcome of government regulation the grimly humorous paradox of a strong Japanese industry competing with a weakened European and American one could be the outcome. Chrysler and British Leyland are already state pensioners. Need pharmaceuticals follow this route? Price and profit controls today would be the harbinger of government subsidy or ownership tomorrow.

NOTES

1. The apparently small absolute UK price rise given these exchange rate variations is due to the equal weighting given to each European currency's dollar value in calculating the value of a 'European' currency unit. Moreover, the British pound was included in the 'European' currency and so appeared in both numerator and denominator of the UK/Europe comparison. The near uniform change of the values of the other three currencies was probably at least in part due to the mechanics of the European Monetary System (EMS) which has existed since March.1979. Britain is not a member of the EMS, a scheme with certain similarities to the pre-1971 IMF fixed-exchange rate system.

REFERENCES

Cooper, M. H. (1966) *Prices and Profits in the Pharmaceutical Industry* (Oxford: Pergamon).

Cooper, M. H. (1975) *European Pharmaceutical Prices* (London: Croom-Helm).

Frisch, R. (1947) in E. Gortz and J. D. Hansen (eds) *Notes in Economic Theory* (Odense).

Von Grebmer, K. (1978) *Pharmaceutical Prices: A Continental View* (London: Office of Health Economics).

Monopolies Commission (1973) *Chlordiazepoxide and Diezepan*, HC 197 (London: HMSO).

National Economic Development Office (NEDO) (1972) *International Price Comparison* (London: HMSO).

Nelson, J. D. E. (1980) 'International Price Comparison', unpublished paper delivered at the American Management Association Seminar, Zurich, 1980.

Polanyi, G. (1973) *Which Way Monopoly Policy?*, Institute of Economic Affairs Research Monograph No. 30 (London: Institute of Economic Affairs).

Reekie, W. D. (1975) *The Economics of the Pharmaceutical Industry* (London: Macmillan).

Reekie, W. D. and M. H. Weber (1979) *Profits, Politics and Drugs* (London: Macmillan).

Royal Canadian Commission on Health (1964) (Ottawa).

Valier, V. (1959) *Comparisons of Prices Charged for Patent Medicines in Italy and Other Countries* (Rome: Pharmindustria).

Valier, V. (1961) *On a Comparison of the Prices of Medicinal Specialities in Italy and Abroad* (Rome: Pharmindustria).

Virts, J. and J. F. Weston (1980) 'Returns to Research and Development in the U. S. Pharmaceutical Industry', *Managerial and Decision Economics*, 1 (3), pp. 103–11.

Index